THE FUNCTION OF THEOLOGY

THE
FUNCTION
OF
THEOLOGY

by

MARTIN THORNTON

HODDER AND STOUGHTON

SBN 340 029811 1

PRINTED IN GREAT BRITAIN FOR HODDER
AND STOUGHTON LIMITED, ST. PAUL'S HOUSE,
WARWICK LANE, LONDON, E.C.4 BY C. TINLING
AND CO. LIMITED, LIVERPOOL, LONDON AND
PRESCOT

To
Dora Chaplin

Editorial Preface

During recent years there has been a remarkable revival of interest in theological studies, covering a wide range of thought and extending to an expanding public. Whatever its underlying causes, this movement has certainly been stimulated by some bold and radical speculation, as well as by a continuing quest for greater personal responsibility in theological decision.

Those responsible for *The Library of Practical Theology* welcome these trends, while recognising that they create new problems and make new demands. Our aim is to try to be of some service in meeting this new situation in a practical way, neither taking sides in current controversy nor forcing any particular viewpoint upon our readers. We hope rather, to assist them to follow their own theological reasoning, and to interpret their own religious experience, with greater clarity. This implies a practical evaluation both of current scholarship and more popular religious thought, which in turn presupposes a certain amount of background historical theology. "A modern re-statement of traditional doctrine" necessitates a sympathetic understanding of what is being re-stated. "Contemporary trends" are hardly intelligible without some study of the historical process from which they have evolved.

A new theological interest having been awakened, we feel that the time is ripe to launch a series of this kind, and we hope that it proves not entirely false to all the implications of its title. We hope that it will develop into a true

Library, a carefully planned corpus of practical studies and not just an interesting collection of books. By *Practical* we mean that which impinges on human experience and makes sense of the present situation. And, while avoiding the heavily technical, the Library will be unashamedly concerned with *Theology.* Our faith is that theology still holds the key to the ultimate meaning of the universe, and as the indispensable interpreter of religious experience, it is still the mainspring of the deepest human fulfilment.

MARTIN THORNTON

Contents

CHAPTER ONE

The Problem

Christian theology today presents a series of curious and exciting paradoxes. While many assume that Christianity is dying a lingering but inevitable death, more theology is being written than ever before. Statistics suggest that active membership of all the Churches is declining, yet theology is being read by a wider public than it has enjoyed since the seventeenth century, and this in proportion to population and literacy: in sheer weight of numbers modern readership in theology is probably greater than it has ever been throughout the history of the Church. Books are pouring from the presses in ever increasing numbers, books of every conceivable type on every imaginable subject, and theology holds its own against this growing competition.

A century ago, when some kind of religious allegiance was considered normal, if not universal, a few of the newly-founded Victorian universities opted out of theology in favour of the new sciences of psychology and sociology. Now, in this "post-Christian age", theology is probably increasing in popularity among students. In all the Churches candidates for the ordained ministry are diminishing—in some cases almost drying up—while in universities where theology has traditionally been taught, the lecture rooms are crowded with young men and women who have no interest in any sort of ecclesiastical

career. Some of these students have deep religious conviction, others have none, yet theology is chosen either in
itself or as part of a general Arts course because it is
found to be interesting. If theology is no longer queen of
the sciences it is proving to be a pretty tough princess who
refuses to be sent into exile. Humanists continue to fight
their crusade against religious instruction in schools, and
they have won a major battle in getting rid of "denominational" teaching—that is teaching other than the academic and historical—which might have practical implications. On the other hand denominational ministers of
religion are now being welcomed into the teaching staffs
of state schools.

"Christendom", whether of medieval or Victorian type,
has gone for good, or at least for several centuries. It has
given way to a culture of "secularity". But this, which
might reasonably be expected to have killed the study of
theology has itself given rise to a vast new theological
movement. Whatever sides churchmen may take, a
theology of the secular is no longer a contradiction in
terms. The modern philosophical movement usually
referred to by the ambiguous word "existentialism" exploded on to the twentieth-century scene with a group of
poets and playwrights of violently anti-religious views.
In the popular mind, existentialism and atheism became
almost synonymous. Now, like the concept of secularity,
existentialism has given rise to a new theological movement. Again, whatever sides churchmen take, there is no
doubt about this revived impetus in the study of theology.

But the ultimate paradox is this: every serious activity
has its theory and its literature, and as activity develops
in practice and complexity its literature grows in proportion. But with Christian theology this ratio would
appear to be reversed: the revival of theological interest
over an ever widening range of readers does not seem to

herald any revival in what is misleadingly called "organised" or "practical" religion. And it certainly does not
spring from it, yet, with the possible exception of a
minority of the philosophically-minded, it is difficult to
see how theology can be of much interest unless it bears
some relation, however tenuous, to human existence. If
gardeners read all the latest journals about gardening or
if cricket enthusiasts spent nostalgic winter evenings
reading books about cricket, it would be curious if the
former never actually did any gardening, or, come May,
the latter blithely carried on reading books without getting anywhere near a cricket ground. But that seems to be
very much the theological position: it is as if the gardening
books were coming out in tens of thousands, and reaching
an ever widening public, while nine houses out of ten were
surrounded by a derelict waste. If Christianity is supposed
to be an activity, something you do, and if the theory of
the thing is so popular, then why are so few people
interested in doing it? So the ultimate paradox leads to
the ultimate question, the question with which this book
and the series it introduces is primarily concerned: What
is theology *for*? How is it supposed to function?

From the complexity of the paradoxes just considered
several answers might be postulated. In the first place it
could be assumed that theology is not *for* anything: it is
an interesting phenomenon in Western culture, a part of
European history, a branch of philosophy, something that
educated people are expected to know something about,
and, in its higher reaches, a subject which keeps a few
professional academicians out of mischief. With the
revival of interest in theology its teaching might, with
some justification, be regarded as a legitimate way of
earning a living. This first viewpoint could then be extended to include the idea that, without allegiance to any
organised religious body or ethic, it is nevertheless of

importance to hold and understand some clear meta-physical belief. Conversely, that if all such belief is rejected it is still of some personal value to know clearly what is rejected and why. It is by no means inconsistent for an atheist or agnostic to retain a genuine interest in theology. In fact it is only the atheist or agnostic who can consistently accept this first interpretation of what theology is for. For those who are not only interested in theology but who come round to accepting its fundamental postulates, in however intellectual a way, must soon find their intellectualism frustrating and unsatisfying. A positive interest in theology must eventually lead to an interest in God, and God can only remain an academic concern to those who doubt his existence.

So secondly, it might be suggested that theology is the necessary theory behind religious practice, that it is the mainspring and directive behind practical Christian living. I believe that this is, ultimately, the correct answer, but two overwhelming objections to it cannot be evaded. The first is that it does not appear to be so: were this the true answer then why does not all the modern interest in theology in all levels of society manifest itself more obviously? The second objection is that if theology is the necessary theory behind Christian practice, then those most nearly concerned with its nurture and propagation do not appear to think so: ministers of religion form a very small proportion of the theology-reading public. There is in fact a multiform rift between theological study and pastoral practice. The pastor is inclined to dismiss the theologian as specialised, unpractical and academic. The scholar appears to have little sympathy with the pastor, and, even in the face of the new interest in theology, is all too apt to discredit "popular" theological writing.

This rift is wider than a direct scholar-pastor opposition. A sincere and zealous Christian layman is bound to believe that Christian practice has a good deal to do with the fight against this world's evils; he must believe with St. Paul that ultimately "we wrestle not against flesh and blood, but against principalities, against powers, against the rulers of the darkness of this world, against spiritual wickedness in the heavenly places". The wealthy layman gladly accepts the duty of almsgiving, and he believes that, at bottom, sin is a far worse scourge than cancer, but he will give liberally towards medical research without even considering the possible claims of theological research. From the strictly Christian point of view he is probably right: the point is that while he does not expect his cheque to solve the cancer problem overnight, he cannot conceive of theological research ever solving any practical problem at all. By implication he is siding with the pastor and parish priest: theology, and especially modern theology, is something practical religion can well do without.

The obverse of this paradox is that all the while "research" in any context becomes a more and more influential "status" word: first-year undergraduates no longer write essays but "theses"; nobody writes a book, they are all "doing research". And it is accepted that medical, scientific, or sociological research is a complicated and long-term project. Our wealthy layman did not expect his cheque, however generous it was, to solve the cancer problem at once: the researchers must be allowed to take their time. But the new theology-reading public, even in the first flush of their enthusiasm, are disappointed when a new book does not conclude with a nice neat answer to a problem. Unlike other researchers, theological scholars are not permitted to take their time; argument and counter-argument, experiment and counter-experiment, scholarly dispute and disagreement, are not seen as part of an unfolding process: "Why cannot the theologians make up their minds?"

Perhaps the new interest in theology is seen simply as of snob-value? Perhaps one should know Tillich, Bonhoeffer and Bishop Robinson to be able to hold one's own in the saloon bar? Or perhaps theology in books is attractive because it deals with a practical matter which most people dislike? The comfort-loving coward usually enjoys tales of high adventure. Or perhaps the agnostic and humanist are studying their foe in order to fight him more ably; perhaps they look with interest at the more radical schools of "secular religion" in the hope that they may prove allies in the end?

Perhaps, on the other hand, there is a deep stirring of religion, a groping after a new conception of spirituality, by those who are dissatisfied with prevailing forms within the Churches? In that case the agnostic and humanist, seeking allies amongst the radical theologians, are likely to be disappointed. This new speculation is more likely to be the beginning of a new research project, which, whatever the initial errors, will get there in the end. But this is a return to our second point: it implies that, somehow or other, by however tortuous a chain of reaction, theology has something to do with religious practice. This again throws up the fundamental question: How? What is theology *for*?

I am not prepared to discount any of the answers here postulated: not even the saloon-bar one. And I am certainly not willing to reject the first possibility that theology is not *for* anything if this means a diminution of its value to the merely pragmatic. Since responsible theology has come round to granting autonomous value to many spheres within a pluralistic secular culture, it can hardly fail to make a similar claim for itself. But this is not the end of the matter: in the nature of the case, incarnational theology cannot be confined within its own specialised boundaries.

So my main purpose in this book is to try to substantiate and explain the more comprehensive view: the theology-practice, chain-reaction ideal. The elaboration of this presents two complications. The first is that the relation between theology and life—if there is one—is a chain-reaction every bit as complicated as in most other modern theory-practice contexts, and it involves more than one intellectual discipline within theology itself. The gardener of our previous analogy may feel justified in laughing at the horticultural expert who, surveying beds of luxuriant blooms, explains why their cultivation is all wrong. But the practical gardener could laugh a little too soon: he already owes more than he thinks to the researchers who have bred the varieties of his roses, and next year his garden might be attacked by all sorts of pests and diseases. Then he will rush in panic to the expert. If our analogy breaks down at any point, it is that our gardens flourish rather more prosperously than our parishes. A more important point is that the gardener is at the practical end of an established chain of relations; the esoteric experiments of the research stations find their results perpetuated in nurseries, seedgrowers, fertiliser manufacturers, and pesticides nicely sealed up in little bottles. Where are the theological nurserymen, seedgrowers and manufacturers? How, in fact, can the fruits of theological research be marketed? It is with this problem that we are to be concerned.

The second complication is even more difficult, although it may contain the key to the whole puzzle. The fruits of scientific research are tangible things of obvious practical value: bottles of insecticide and boxes of pills. The fruits of philosophy may well impinge upon human history, but they are basically books: books which are deemed to have

B

fulfilled their purpose when they are read and understood. Theology is different: it cannot issue in an end-product like a pill, yet it is assumed to be more practical than philosophy. Theology cannot be said to have fulfilled its final purpose when it is just understood; the most specialised scholar generally assumes that it should have some practical impact on the outward life of those who understand and accept it. With the existentialist outlook, moreover, theology is assumed to concern the whole of human life in the most practical way: it is concerned with total experience in a total situation. A pill is successful if it relieves a particular pain, ethics are successful if they improve human behaviour, but theology cannot claim to be practical unless it changes, or develops, or improves a complete human being, together with his total environment. A scientific chain of reaction may be simply put: laboratory-chemist-doctor-pill-patient. Its theological equivalent would have to include some all-embracing relationship between each successive stage; some comprehensive catalyst which would cause the necessary reactions between the stages and which would link together all those concerned in the process into a comprehensive pattern.

This common factor which renders theology of use, and which should run through the whole process from specialised scholar to believing peasant, is, I maintain, *prayer within the Church:* but here we have to be very careful indeed. If prayer can be defined as the living relation between man and God then it is at the very peak of human experience and the greatest of human values which cannot be made subservient to anything else— however "practical". It is a travesty of Christian prayer to put its value in terms of self-culture or moral improvement. It must also be understood that, although ascetical theology is a complicated subject treating of prayer according to types, scales, methods and values, the simple prayer of Christian people—their everyday petitions and intercessions—is also a supreme value in its own right, and this irrespective of theology or practical "results". Nevertheless, having made this point as clear as I can, I wish, for the purpose in hand to push it into the background. Prayer does, in fact, produce fruits, even if this is not its prime value and point, and it does do a great deal for the personality, even if this is not the greatest of its fruits. Prayer has something to do with "self-culture", but only if this is accepted as an insignificant by-product and prayer is practised in a spirit of acquired self-forgetfulness.

The point is that theology can never be of practical use without prayer, but I passionately disclaim any suggestion that rendering theology useful is the purpose of prayer: theology should serve prayer, not vice versa. Nevertheless, prayer renders theology of practical use in both direct and indirect ways. Directly, because a man reading, understanding and even being excited by a simple book of popular theology, will gain no practical benefit until its theology has been absorbed and applied by prayer of an "intellectual-meditation" type. Indirectly, because the full implications of theology, especially modern theology, will never be grasped by the intellect alone. An understanding of a popular book will depend on spiritual intuitions and insights which are, in fact, by-products nurtured by the full implications of a Christian life of prayer. If the popular book is of any real value these intuitions and insights will have played their part in its production from more scholarly sources. But again beware! The opening out of the personality to the spirituality of the universe, the development of spiritual insight, intuition, prophecy, intellectual sensitivity, contemplative perception—all this is inevitable by-product of prayer but God forbid that it should be regarded as anything more. Prayer cannot be relegated to a system of psychological education.

This is not pietism. The centrality of prayer is not just a devout ideal but an integral part of the current theological movement itself. The significance to modern theology of existentialism, of linguistic philosophy, of new approaches to biblical scholarship, and of the reaction against legalist ethics—all this militates against a theology reduced to the historical and intellectual. Modern theology is forced to embrace concepts like faith, insight, speculative spirituality and religious experience: all fruits of prayer. Apart from the importance of this in terms of theological function, it renders obsolete any attempts at "non-denominational" teaching. Serious prayer must spring from some systematic theology which includes doctrines of grace, baptism, and the Church, and in the nature of the case this must be tied with a "denomination". The idea of a professor of theology with no personal religious conviction—as recently suggested by the University of Lancaster—is regarded by its supporters as broad-minded, ecumenical and objective, and by its opponents as impious. What is not generally realised is that such a concept is at least half a century out of date.

There is one further point of the utmost consequence: although the absorption and use of theology through prayer is directly related to contemplation, prayer itself can no longer (if it ever could) be treated in terms of a single, isolated method or type. It is barely permissible to speak of *a* prayer as an isolated unit, and it is usually disastrous to assess the "results" of single prayers or periods of prayer in terms of success or failure. Prayer must be seen as a theological complex of life, a spiritual and recollective continuum made up of a totality of prayers, offices, meditations, liturgical actions and the rest. It is an overall pattern of life, a system, or to use the technical term, a *regula*. It is only from such a total commitment to a spiritual life that the gifts of insight and discernment can develop. And such development is usually a gradual process which proceeds by grace irrespective of any clear "results" of the contemplation of truth on particular occasions. If therefore, these qualities of insight and discernment are to be nurtured I make no excuse for spending a considerable part of this book in a re-examination of regula from this special viewpoint. It becomes the key, not only to a possible modern spirituality, but also to the creative use of all theology, or even a true understanding of theology. Conversely, if a modern theologian rejects the pattern of the traditional regula, then he cannot replace it by a new "method" of prayer. It can only be replaced by another complete trinitarian *system*, which, so far as I know, does not exist.

It is regrettable that if prayer and theology are drawing closer in academic circles, this relation is still disregarded in pastoral and personal religion. Theology is still seen either as something useless or as something to be *taught* not *used*. Yet there is some excuse for this attitude for specialised scholarship cannot be used without a chain of mediation which is at present lacking. One purpose of this series is an attempt to supply this need.

Nevertheless this "modern" and "scholarly" insistence on faith, insight and discernment as necessary to theology is no new thing in pastoral practice. It has long been obvious that men cannot be argued into faith in creeds; they believe or they do not, their eyes see and their ears hear or they do not: something more than persuasive logic is required. To return full circle I cannot but think that this provides an important key to the understanding of modern theological controversy. With respect, and I hope humility, it seems that the exciting battle between orthodoxy and radical theology is, at bottom, an encounter between those who discern through a continuum of prayer and those who would put all their theological eggs into one intellectual basket. The "supranatural" is a discernible possibility or a brick wall: you cannot argue about it. This is not to deny all sincerity or devotion to the latter group; it means that they have themselves denied that specifically orthodox scheme of prayer which "opens the eyes" on spiritual and supranatural things. The "demythologising" approach to the New Testament, for example, is no doubt a valid and valuable aspect of modern scholarship. But it started with the assumption that the biblical myths, parables, analogies and poems were incomprehensible to modern man. The real truth is that they are incomprehensible to any man of any age who has not developed a spiritual discernment by prayer and who cannot use them in prayer. No doubt most people today come into this group but it is not a specifically modern problem. To do away with myth and translate the New Testament into contemporary terms is of much value as a preliminary step, but it only solves an intellectual problem which modern theology itself declares to be insufficient. It might be more constructive, and more modern, to concentrate on the existential *use* of the New Testament rather than on its "meaning".

A discussion between orthodoxy, "conservatism" if you will, and radical thought on, for example, the existence of angels, usually ends with the same brick wall as was found in pastoral frustration: you cannot argue about angels except on a mundane historical and philosophical plane. The possibility, or probability of their existence within an unseen realm can, or cannot, be discerned. When the radical secularist's opponent is a learned man the former is bewildered, when an "ignorant" man then he speaks of superstition and credulity: but the reason for genuine faith in angels is, ultimately, the same in both cases. It is a matter of discernment.

The same position applies to most of the "difficulties" of modern theology: to the Virgin Conception, the physical Ascension, Christian morality, and so on. All these are subjects of scholarship, their historical setting and philosophical interpretation are important, but the only "answer" to these problems is to learn how to *use*, or try to use them as the raw material, the initial spark, of meditative and contemplative prayer.

But I have readily admitted that this is not simple; it needs the working out of a set of theological relations before it can work: before theology can properly function.

CHAPTER TWO

Five Functions of Theology

From the practical point of view, Christianity begins with the confrontation between Jesus Christ and the chosen twelve. To the apostles, and then to all who met Jesus, this was a religious experience of awe, excitement, questioning and bewilderment. It was also Christian prayer—of which the confrontation of men by Christ is a working definition—and we should not be surprised when our own prayer and thought are characterised by awe, excitement, questioning and bewilderment. This experience of confrontation becomes more complex, and more bewildering, as the great events of the gospel unfold. More and more questioning arose as the disciples witnessed the Passion, Crucifixion, Resurrection and Ascension, and as they lived through the tremendous experience of Pentecost.

Through all the vicissitudes of speculation and argument which characterised the life of the Church in the first centuries, there finally evolved a series of formulae: questioning experience was crystallised into dogma and creed. The purpose of this body of theology was, at first, to guide each new generation of Christians into a proper interpretation of its own experience of confrontation with the risen Christ. Theology and prayer—according to our initial definition—both become more complicated: the former widens the scope of the latter. Confrontation

FIVE FUNCTIONS OF THEOLOGY   25

with Christ may still be a simple awareness of his presence according to some image or symbol. This issues in personal dialogue or colloquy which is what is normally if ambiguously meant by "mental prayer", that is an interchange between minds: the mind of man with the mind of Christ. This is how the "voice of God" is verily "heard" by the spiritual ears of the dedicated mind. If this is the heart of Christian life it is neither its peak nor its totality: confrontation with the risen Christ means infinitely more than the individualistic idea of "Christ as personal Saviour". Theology leads on to a richer confrontation of a corporate nature; to the relation involved in baptismal incorporation —of being ontologically "in Christ"—and to a deepening awareness of the eucharistic presence. Confrontation with Christ thus expands into his indwelling of humanity and of nature, and to further colloquy with the word revealed in Scripture. Finally, the central doctrines of the Holy Trinity, of Christology, of the Church and the Atonement further rebound to the elaboration of prayer into a total continuum of life in all its aspects.

That true faith leads into action, that doctrine is to be expressed in practical life, are truisms. It is also obvious that as the Church develops into an organic complex, spreading throughout the world and spanning the centuries, its theology and practice become more specialised: problems and opportunities are both multiplied, theology splits up into sections and sub-sections, spirituality becomes diversified into a rich pattern of schools and traditions according to age and culture. This complexity makes it all the more necessary to try to discern some functional pattern in theology as a whole. Prayer remains the unifying force since prayer is indissociable from the Holy Spirit of unity, harmony and wholeness. But there must still be a pattern if we are to avoid the prevailing confusion caused by the current disintegrated jumble of minutely specialised studies. The overall question is the concern of all Christian people, and may be of value and interest to non-Christians as well. Both the divinity professor and the faithful peasant, the popular preacher and the confirmation candidate, are ultimately concerned with this prior question: What is theology all about? What is it for?

As a preliminary hypothesis, I suggest that the total complex of theology may be discerned under five inter-related heads, modes or functions. These may briefly be set out as follows.

First, theology has a prior *revelational* function; the disclosure and proclamation of revealed knowledge.

Second is *practical* or *straight* theology, the implications of which are obvious and which necessitate a spontaneous reaction.

Third is *pastoral* theology, or that which is employed by Christian pastors in ministering to their flocks. Pastoral theology, as a subject of study, means the drawing out of the practical implications of theological statements and formulae.

Fourth is *applied* theology, sometimes called *ascetic* theology, which guides, or is used to guide, individual Christians in their uniquely personal interpretation of discipleship, according to temperament and circum-stances.

Fifth is what I should call the *negative* or *testing* function of theology, which guards people and communities from error in prayer, and therefore in practical life.

If this scheme is to be given the chance to make any sense of the present situation it must ever be borne in mind that we are thinking of relations forged by prayer, not of rigid distinctions. There must be a good deal of overlap between the five modes or functions, if only because practical living is never all that tidy. If, moreover, these

five suggested headings are not allowed to react one upon
the others, then we are further enmeshed in that sterile
departmentalism we are trying to overcome. To clarify
this point the scheme might be put in another way.

I have been careful to give an autonomous value to
prayer because it is the activity of the whole man in his
relation to God. If "spirituality", or the "spiritual life",
concerns the whole of life in grace with prayer as its mainspring, then it is true to speak of prayer as life in its
spiritual mode, as total human activity in its religious
mode. What I have been careful to avoid is the idea of
religion, prayer or spirituality as a useful addenda to
some other kind of life. But this does not prevent us from
considering the various ways in which prayer can function
in its practical interpretation of theology to the general
enrichment of life. The same sort of argument also applies
to other aspects of the Christian life which play their part
in the totality of prayer. Liturgy is life in a particular
mode; music is worship in a particular mode. Liturgy is
not just an isolated piece of religiosity, and music is not
simply an addendum to liturgy. All this means is that
biblical and Christian psychology is taken seriously: man
is an integrated unity not a collection of faculties. Thus
William of St. Thierry, following the mainstream of
biblical tradition, speaks of the threefold division of
personality, *anima, animus, spiritus*, not as "faculties" but
as modes or activities of the whole integrated being.

This reasoning also applies to theology. If *animus* is the
whole person in the process of reasoning, then theology is
religion in its cognitive mode; it is the Christian faith
from this particular point of view. It follows that theology
must also be granted its autonomous value, but, as in the
prior case of prayer, this does not invalidate our consideration as to how it can function, or how it can be used,
in Christian practice. The error is the failure to see

theology as an activity of the whole man within the Church, which is apt to reduce it to a sterile intellectualism. To see theology as, in the proper sense, functional, is not to depreciate its intrinsic value but to enrich it.

It is this insistence of an autonomy in theology that leads to its prior *revelational* function. If we believe that the incarnate life of Jesus Christ reveals truths that cannot be discerned in any other way, then it is the duty of the theologians of the Church to proclaim it. Theology speaks to the world, and must speak to the world, whether or not the world is disposed to receive its gospel. The "academic" error is not to insist upon this point but to stop with it, failing to see that theology has, in fact, much pragmatic significance in many subtle ways. But this is not the false pragmatism of Roman Catholic modernism. Practicality can never be a test of the validity of revealed truth, but this does not mean that revealed truth has no practical consequences. In fact, a good deal of the revealed and proclaimed gospel calls forth an immediate practical response, and this is what I have called *practical* or *straight* theology. That the attitude of God towards men is not that of tyrant, despot or taskmaster, but of father, is a proclamation which, received through a discerning ear, must immediately change a man's whole attitude to life.

But it is an extension of the "academic" error—which, it needs hardly saying, is not confined to academicians— to assume that all theology, or even most of it, is of this type. A major proportion of Christian doctrine calls forth little or no immediate response. This does not mean that it has no practical bearing on human life but rather that its living significance has to be drawn out by further thought, and then mediated to faithful people. This process I have called *pastoral* theology. Conversely, a Christian community of a specific culture at a particular age, will be confronted by its own problems and aspirations. It will grope after the implications of revealed truth upon these local and contemporary factors. Such searching through prayer—which always includes a cognitive element—is also pastoral theology. But the interaction between this third function with the prior revelational aspect of theology helps us to keep these two aspects of pastoral theology in the right order. True pastoral theology is concerned not so much with "adapting theology to modern circumstances" but with accepting an existential situation and then attempting an honest assessment of what revealed truth has to say about it. Needless to say, such an assessment is only possible through an interaction between theology and prayer.

Circumstances, aspirations and problems, however, pertain not only to ages and cultures but to individual people. The corporate proclamation of theology and pastoral theology needs further interpretation to men and women in their unique situations. This is *applied* or *ascetic* theology, known to Christian tradition as spiritual direction or personal guidance in prayer and morals.

As background to the whole scheme, and interacting with each function in turn, is *negative* or *testing* theology. It is the obverse side of the first which underlines the positive value of understanding heresy. Theological students are wont to complain that after three years of doctrinal studies they have only learned what the faith is not. Even if this were true it would not be wholly without pastoral value, and if we all took heresy more seriously a good deal of modern frustration would be avoided. To convinced Christian people humanistic ethics can be made to sound very plausible: until they collapse in the light of the doctrines of grace and of teleology. The prayer, and therefore the lives, of devout people are often tragically inhibited because of an insufficient Christology. Many a priest, however sincere and zealous, suffers agonies of frustration because of an unexamined dualism based on an erroneous convention: his priesthood and his manhood are perpetually in conflict, which is another Christological problem. Much pastoral activity, ecclesiastical and secular, ends in frustrated failure because it is sincere, well-meaning, enthusiastic, and—unknown and un-detected—heretical. A great deal of useless energy would be saved if every new scheme, programme or policy was first tested, and passed, by *negative, testing* theology.

If this scheme is seen against the present theological situation, it will be apparent that the first, *revelational* or autonomous outlook is that generally held by the leading scholars. The last, however neglected it has become, is nevertheless tacitly assumed by a good many practical pastors to be their sole use for theology: simply to guard against error. This is really a *negative* concept, while this fifth theological function *in its association with the rest* becomes a much more positive value. It is with the third and fourth uses of theology, the *pastoral* and *applied*, that we shall be mainly concerned in this book, because they contain the key to the enrichment of the others, and because they would appear to be the most neglected. Before proceeding with the examination of these two central concepts, however, it is necessary to look a little more closely at the second category, particularly in its relation to prayer within the living, concrete situation. For this purpose it is as well to return to its origins.

Confronted by Jesus Christ, the disciple faces certain questions and experiences emotions of frighteningly practical significance. These questions and experiences multiply and deepen before they are resolved: Who and what is this extraordinary man? Is he Messiah, or a prophet, or more than a prophet? By what authority does he do these things? Is he to be obeyed, or followed, or trusted? And to what extent: in a thoughtful and prudent way or

generously, without reserve? The answers to these practical questions ultimately depend on the answer to the
initial one: Who is this? And this prior question cannot be
answered entirely in a cool logical way, although at
bottom it is an intellectual question. It cannot finally be
divorced from the emotions of awe and excitement arising
from the personality of Jesus: "never man spake like this
man." St. Matthew tells us with an almost childlike simplicity that as the holy women "went to tell his disciples,
behold, Jesus met them, saying, All hail. And they came
and held him by the feet, and worshipped him". This
sounds like a spontaneous reaction, a deep feminine
intuitive act of adoration, but it must either have arisen
from, or given rise to, a good deal of rational heart-
searching. Devout Jewish women can *adore* God only, and
here was a man, a resurrected man indeed but a man
nevertheless; or was he more than man? Was he divine,
and if so was he God? And if so were there two Gods?
Was he indeed man, or was the human appearance some
sort of phantasm? "Behold my hands and my feet, that
it is I myself: handle me, and see; for a spirit hath not
flesh and bones, as ye see me have." But how can a man
be God at the same time? In *The Shape of Christology*,
John McIntyre pertinently asks: "The questions with
which the liturgical interest will always tax any christological analysis will, therefore, be: How easily does the
analysis integrate with a living situation in which the
believer trusts, loves and obeys Jesus Christ? To what
degree is the analysis organically united with the worship
of Christ, so that it finally comes to inform, to deepen and
enrich the worship of Christ? This is the final test of any
christology . . ."

So all these questions, springing from the minds of
simple disciples, arose from an intensely practical need;
a straightforward decision had to be made: may we, or

may we not, worship and adore this person? On the other hand it needs no great theological acumen to see in these questions the seeds of four and a half centuries of controversy ending in the Church's dogmatic trinitarian and Christological formulae. The questions, asked by simple disciples in the living experience of confrontation with the risen Christ, had to be answered. They must continually be answered and, if need be, reinterpreted for the guidance of simple disciples throughout the ages. They are difficult questions fully extending the best theological minds the Church can produce, then and now, and the resultant doctrine is of an intricacy far beyond the powers of ordinary people to grasp. But ordinary Christians still need the results of all this theological controversy, they need the basic answers, and these answers are still practical or straight theology. As with Magdalene and Mary the mother of James and Joses, the real question is still the practical one: not so much the substantive "What is the relation between the divine and human natures in the Person of Christ?" but the existential "Can we both freely commune with and yet adore the God-man?" At this stage the more intricate formulae which gives the Church's mandate to answer emphatically "yes" need not bother the simple believer, but this more developed theology remains of everyday use to him when interpreted as pastoral, or as applied, theology.

So it is with the doctrine of the Church, the eucharist, and practically all of the simple, straightforward statements of the creeds. Pentecost was, pre-eminently, a staggering spiritual experience, the implications of which took centuries to formulate. The doctrine of the Church is still a matter of controversy but whatever theory is accepted by a serious Christian, it is bound to have an immediate effect on his outlook towards his fellow Christians and on his life in general. It is straight theology.

So is eucharistic doctrine, again of whatever type. Our
Lord's action and command in the upper room left the
apostles bewildered. It needed Emmaus to drive the point
home, and several more centuries to achieve some intellectual explanation of it. Once again the controversy
continues but whatever tradition is clearly taught to the
ordinary believer, and simply accepted by him, immediately dictates his attitude to it and his approach to
eucharistic worship.

At one stage removed from this immediate response to
theology, yet still under this general heading of practical
or straight doctrine, is what, following the ascetical
teaching of William of St. Thierry, may be called
"absorbed" theology or "internal" faith. This means that
a credal statement, although it may exercise no immediate
or spontaneous reaction on the life of one who receives it
nevertheless becomes "absorbed" into his personality by
reflection and contemplation. Such reflection does not
imply any high intellectual ability or sustained study, but
rather a simple conscious attention to the fact itself. I
suggest that, in ordinary Christian life, the doctrines of
the Atonement and of divine providence come under this
heading. The ideas that, somehow or other, forgiveness
of sins is made possible by the sacrifice of Christ on the
Cross, or that, somehow or other and come what may,
the love of the Father is active in every situation in life,
may not immediately make much practical sense to
ordinary people. But these doctrinal facts gradually reveal
their meaning to simple believers living normally within
the Church and assisted by grace.

This "absorption" of faith is, in technical spiritual
theology, a contemplative rather than an intellectual
process, but it is a mistake to understand these two
categories as mutually exclusive. Contemplation is usually
regarded as something apart from discursive reasoning,

c

but all contemplation allows of some intellectual element, and the thinking out of doctrine, on however lowly a plane, is a religious value which assists the absorption of faith. If we follow the tradition of St. Augustine and St. Anselm, faith precedes understanding—*credo ut intellegam;* nevertheless the same tradition insists that understanding, the pursuit of theological studies, ought to rebound to the strengthening of faith. Although great intellectual ability is not necessary to faith, and although all theological findings should be practically usable in one of the five ways we are proposing, divine learning and the practice of Christian living ought to grow in proportion. That this is not always the case is, I believe, one of the regrettable results of a misunderstanding of the real practicality of theology itself.

I suggest that the hard core of this misunderstanding is to be found in the restriction of the use of theology to this simple first category, and to the consequent neglect of pastoral, and then of applied, theology. A frightening amount of current theological work falls into one of two groups: it is either "scholarship" or it is "popular". The former is assumed to be of interest to a small coterie of highly specialised professionals with no practical consequences to the Church at large. In a few cases at least it is assessed in terms of the furtherance of the author's personal career which is again assumed to have no bearing on the mission of the Church. The whole thing is liable to degenerate into an esoteric little game. It is this attitude which causes a breakdown in the Anselmic principle that learning, holiness and practical Christian living should interact and progress together. I must make the point, however, that the fault for this state of affairs is by no means all on the side of the scholars in question. The fault lies rather in the general neglect of pastoral and applied theology which should forge a creative link between scholar and pastor and then between pastor and his flock. Within the whole Church all three groups may justly be held culpable for failing to forge the necessary relationships. Medical research cannot be blamed if the general practitioner discounts its findings and patients distrust the general practitioner.

"Popular" theology on the other hand is invariably assumed to be of the practical or straight kind; it is optimistically hoped that once read through, the practical life of ordinary Christians will automatically change for the better. But theology of this type is restricted to the plainest doctrinal statements; I would say to the statements of the Apostles' Creed and perhaps to the very simplest expositions of them. In practice, more especially as education and healthy questioning develop, things are more complex. A convert may start with the practical fact that since Christ is both God and man he may be worshipped and also approached freely in prayer. But the modern convert will soon ask, again for very practical reasons, whether Christ is really a mixture of God and man or whether he is two persons alternating between the divine and human. His attempt to follow out the Christian life will land him in the intricate problems of Christology. He will need the assistance of his pastor; straight theology has expanded into pastoral theology. Or the change of outlook immediately following the acceptance of the fact of divine providence may subtly and slowly degenerate into pagan fatalism, or to determinism. Again the straight fact of divine providence needs to be elaborated into pastoral theology.

Further, a group of Christians guided by a competent pastor and growing in faith within the worshipping fellowship, will eventually develop individual problems arising out of personal circumstances and temperament. Each Christian is a unique person with his own difficulties and with his own particular gifts: in its turn pastoral theology needs to be *applied* personally to particular cases. The final stage is *ascetical* theology, which includes moral casuistry, with *negative* theology in the background as a necessary safeguard against error.

CHAPTER THREE

Pastoral Theology

The distinction between pastoral and applied theology is admittedly artificial; in practice the division becomes blurred but it is still a useful one for purposes of analysis and clarification. Traditionally, pastoral theology means that adaptation of doctrine by the pastor in the general oversight of his flock, and here the pastor is synonymous with the parish priest. Applied or ascetical theology denotes a more specialised skill in adapting doctrine to the spiritual and moral needs of individual people in their particular circumstances. Obviously both uses may be employed by one person in his pastoral work and our immediate task is to trace the development of these more complex functions from straight theology, as well as to discuss the various relationships involved within the total life of the Church. We shall then consider how this double process of development and relationship must continue to evolve if the needs of the twentieth-century Church are to be met.

As well as a necessary development with the deepening of faith, and growing from a healthy questioning of faith, the progression from straight to pastoral and pastoral to applied theology is also an historical one. In the New Testament the practical problems of confrontation with Jesus Christ were mostly solved by spiritual intuition: a bold decision was made and the questioning followed.

Matthew left his job and just went; Magdalene and Mary witnessed the resurrected Christ and just worshipped. Then came the questions and the need for pastoral theology which at its simplest meant the teaching of one man on two levels, the work of a composite theologian-pastor. St. Paul adopts this method in a good many of the epistles: the proclamation of a straight doctrinal fact is followed by some further exposition and then by its practical implications.

The next stage in the process was a division of labour between scholar and pastor. As theology developed and the Church expanded there arose men of special intellectual gifts and spiritual insight whose job it was to examine, speculate upon and unravel the intricate theological questions thrown up by the experience of the worshipping community. The distinction is still blurred: the scholar may be, and frequently was, a pastor as well, but it was now assumed that the more vocational pastor would read his works and interpret his conclusions in the guidance of his flock. It is roughly the relation between St. Paul and Timothy.

The final stage (historically speaking, but not, I think, the final stage in its sufficiency to meet twentieth-century needs) is that in which the distinction between scholar and pastor becomes so marked that any creative liaison between them demands the work of an intermediary: the pastoral theologian. This is the notorious gap between scholarship and pastoral practice which has been a diabolical problem, certainly in Anglicanism, since the seventeenth century. It remains with us in a new and very complex form, but it is important to realise that it is, at bottom, no new problem. It at least helps towards a sane perspective to remember that if the modern pastor feels frustrated by some of the intricate arguments of current theological speculation, his fourth-century counterpart in some remote Cappadocian village must have been equally bewildered by the writings of St. Gregory of Nazianzus. Since that time the pastoral theologian has been the necessary and recognised go-between. The modern scholar may have little pastoral sense, the modern pastor may have little taste for theology—which is regrettable all round—but it is useless to hark back to simpler times when the two functions were normally combined in one man. It is equally useless to aim at the ideal wherein all scholars and all pastors are Pauls, Augustines and Anselms. A case could be made in support of this fourfold relationship—scholar, pastoral theologian, pastor, people —as intrinsic to the normal functioning of the organic body of Christ. It is a pastoral analogue of the ministerial division of bishop, priest, deacon, and laity, and I would tentatively suggest that it has a similar biblical basis.

"Now you are Christ's body, and each of you a limb or organ of it. Within our community God has appointed, in the first place apostles, in the second place prophets, thirdly teachers; then miracle workers, then those who have gifts of healing, or ability to help others or power to guide them" (I Cor. 12. 27–8 N.E.B.). It is to be expected that elsewhere (e.g. Rom. 12. 6–8; Acts 13. 1) these distinctions change and overlap, and it would be a little far-fetched—as well as beyond my own competence—to try to substantiate this hypothesis in detail. Yet there would appear to be some correspondence: apostles are not only the authoritative Church rulers who proclaim the hard facts of the faith, but also, according to St. Paul's own definition, those who have "seen the Lord"; who have experienced the initial confrontation with Christ. Prophets are those of marked spiritual insight, who have also, again like St. Paul, seen the Lord in the confrontation of contemplative prayer or mystical experience. Together, as in Acts 13. 1, prophets and teachers could mean the inspired and gifted thinker, the original scholar, while in 1 Corinthians 12. 30 and 14. 5 St. Paul speaks of the need to "interpret", and in 14. 6 of the need to speak "either by revelation, or by knowledge, or by prophesying, or by doctrine". The teacher and interpreter would appear to be very like my pastoral theologian, mediating theology to those with "ability to help others or power to guide them", that is, to the vocational pastor. I would not press the exposition. The overall point is that if we are seriously to consider the uses of theology in Christian practice we must accept this complex of relationship within the body of Christ, while granting autonomous value to each function. It is right for all Christians to recognise their membership one of another within the body, to see their particular gifts as of the body, and to respect each special vocation, but the scholar must be allowed to pursue his researches—however specialised and esoteric they may be—without reference to their obvious or immediate practicality. The uses of his results are the concern of the pastor, helped if need be by the pastoral theologian. "Are all apostles? are all prophets? are all teachers? do all interpret?" The current, and indeed perennial problem is not so much in the specialisation of the scholar or in the incompetence of the pastor but in the rift between them, largely occasioned by the absence of the pastoral theologian.

The role of the pastoral theologian, however, now and throughout the ages, is itself more complex than the simple idea of "interpreter" suggests. It has varied and must vary according to age and circumstance: with trends and fashions in theological studies, the intellectual gap between scholar and pastor, and spiritualities and ecclesiastical discipline current in different times and places. While the Church's scholars were concerned with Trinitarian, Christological, and Atonement doctrine, or with ascetical and moral theology, their findings were reasonably close to the practical needs of ordinary Christians. In such ages the scholar and pastoral theologian were intimately related and not infrequently combined in one man: Gregory of Nazianzus, John Chrysostom, Ambrose, Augustine, and Gregory the Great all wrote a good deal of "occasional", catechetical, or pastoral theology. So, in like manner, did Taylor, Sanderson, Hooker, Beveridge, and Burnet, with many others of the English seventeenth century. On the other hand when scholars were concerned with the number of angels that could stand on the point of a pin, or with philosophical deism, and perhaps even with certain aspects of biblical criticism, then the scholar-pastor relation is more tenuous.

The intrinsic intellectual ability between scholar and pastor has also varied throughout Christian history, and indeed with—if the term is permissible—Christian geography. It is conceivable that Paul and Titus, scholar and pastor, spoke and thought on equal terms. So did Bernard of Clairvaux and Gilbert of Sempringham. Many a seventeenth-century English country parson appreciated the works of the great Caroline scholars. In all these situations the pastor's flock, whatever their intellectual attainments, would have accepted a good deal of personal responsibility in religion and would have been exhorted to experiment in applying Christian principles to their prayer and their lives.

At other times the intellectual scholar-pastor gap widened until any sort of constructive communication was impossible. The pastoral theologian is then reduced to offering the simplest rule-of-thumb guidance in the form of manual and penitentiary. This situation applied throughout most of the middle ages, a period of unparalleled theological insight, both mystical and scholastic, yet in the pastoral hands of a semi-literate priesthood. Although an over-simplication, this period was characterised by a largely affective spirituality rightly controlled by an authoritarian ecclesiastical regime. Practical Christian living consisted in obedience to the priest while the priest's orders were culled from manual and penitentiary. No doubt the fruits of the great theological achievement of the age seeped through to the pastoral level in some measure, but by and large it seems unlikely that the work of Anselm, Aquinas or Bonaventure could have made much *immediate* impact on ordinary daily life. A further factor in the presentation of pastoral theology is the varying emphasis on community and individuality. In I Corinthians 12, St. Paul gives a sublime account of how in ideal Christian practice the two coincide and support one another: a proper submission to the corporate body advances rather than frustrates unique personality, and the most gifted prophet finds his pioneering of new ways supported by a common discipline and liturgy. But the ideal is hard to achieve; throughout history the emphasis has shifted back and forth from "diversities of gifts" to the "unity of the body". While it is absurd to regard the middle ages as a period of unrelieved regimentation, and sillier still to see monasticism as a system aimed at crushing individuality, nevertheless the common discipline of the Church had been largely in the ascendant up to the Reformation period. This means pastoral theology rather than ascetical or applied theology, which in the modern age comes more and more into its own. Before considering this question, however, we may well pause to see how the modern situation compares with the historical fluctuations just considered.

Theological vogue today covers so great a range that it is impossible to generalise about its practical significance, but there are certain main trends which suggest a return from academics to a more pastoral approach. Biblical studies may seem, at first sight, to continue in a rarefied atmosphere, especially in Germany, yet the whole concept of "biblical theology" has a close relation to practical spirituality and therefore with Christian living. In that vast realm commonly called "philosophical theology" the emphasis is on language, with its obvious connection with the communication of religious truth, and with existential interpretation of dogma: a plainly practical approach compared with the categories of scholasticism and the substantive facts of older credal formulae. It is also significant that with the paperback revolution and popular interest, more and more professional scholars are occasionally branching out into pastoral, or "popular" exposition. We are in some way returning to the patristic and Caroline fashion wherein serious and creative thinkers are almost expected to produce some equivalent to the catechetical commentary. Studies in the so-called "new theology", serious thought and writing about "secularisation" (as against a panic-stricken opposition to the "secular" of recent times) would be impossible or ignored without a real renewal of pastoral interest. Moreover the very idea of a workable relation between the Christian and the secular has opened up a vast new order of practical theological thought. The breakdown of "Christendom", and more important the calm acceptance of its breakdown, is a tremendous stimulus to serious pastoral thought. The new sciences of psychology and sociology might now become firmly married to theology instead of taking on the aspect of appendages. Whatever the difficulties involved there looks like real hope that pastoral theology and practice must soon become emancipated from the pathetic puerilities to which it has been chained for half a century.

What of the gap between the modern scholar and

pastor? At first sight it would appear to be enormous, possibly wider than ever before, and in some respects this is a true judgement. But I do not think it need be, and I do not think it can continue to be. Whatever the width of the gap, it springs from a new situation which necessitates some bold new thought about the role of pastoral theology in the modern world. Such difference as there is arises not so much from the innate intellectual capacities of scholar and pastor but from the specialisation of theological studies. The intrinsic difference between the modern specialist scholar and the non-graduate parish priest, not to mention the growing band of theologically-concerned lay people, is nowhere near so wide as that between Aquinas and his contemporary village priests. The trouble is the absence of the true pastoral theologian which, I have been bold to suggest, is not merely a second-rate scholar but a Christian of spiritual insight with a quite specific vocation within the economy of the body of Christ. Without him, the pastor gives up hope—with every excuse—of understanding specialised theology, and sinks back into the conventional puerilities. The modern pastor becomes a new anomaly: one with the medieval manual-penitentiary outlook yet one equipped with very much more than a peasant-priest intellect.

Specialisation, however, presents new problems for the would-be pastoral theologian. Until fairly recently, the pastoral theologian, without unduly great gifts of learning, could be expected to understand scholarly productions in most branches of divine learning and interpret their trends and results in practical terms. Today the pastoral theologian, with that vocation but with average gifts, cannot possibly be expected to keep up with more than one particular branch of specialised study. If the Church in the past was well served by pastoral theology, this aspect of its mission now needs its own specialists: we have to think in terms of pastoral-biblical theology; pastoral-dogmatic theology; pastoral-philosophical theology and so on. This implies no less than a reorientation of the whole realm of theological scholarship and education. The possibility has been investigated by Karl Rahner in the narrower context of training for the priesthood. But what he says is expandable into the wider realm of practical theology: "During the last century and a half, if the priest was to make any impact he had to be 'educated', meaning *academically* educated. But what this meant was that he had to be scientifically educated in the sense that applies to a modern university and its organization of research and specialization. Thus it was as a reflection of the general shape of things in the secular intellectual world that modern theological studies arose ... But the meaning and limitations of academic study in the university have now arrived at a critical point: the *universitas litterarum* is bursting apart under the pressure of endless subdivisions; it is in danger of becoming a mere blanket organization for a number of specialist schools; what it provides is gradually becoming a mere specialist training for 'technicians' in individual sciences." Then, more succinctly to our purpose: "If what Catholic theology is doing is not training expert specialists in a science, but training priests, i.e. men called by God to be pastors (in secular terms, leaders), then the fact that academically trained people are no longer assumed to be the born leaders of the people must provide theology with particular food for thought." (*Mission and Grace*, vol. II, vii, pp. 148–50.) Rahner goes on to plead for a division of approach to theological training, the academic and the pastoral, but insists that this should be seen not as a double standard but as two distinct disciplines of equal value. This scheme, sound as it is, shows up the present lack of anything that can be regarded as a pastoral theological corpus. I know from personal experience that in the training of potentially first-rate pastors of but average intellectual ability, not to mention the guidance of influential lay people, one is forced to search for "simple" academic books for their use. Such "simple" academic books are frequently, though not always, second-rate scholarship. The need is not for "simple" second-rate academic theology but for first-rate pastoral theology, and the only *basis* for this is first-class scholarship.

The reorientation needed in the total realm of divine learning can, therefore, be stated quite simply and then elaborated almost indefinitely. The simple need is for the fourfold division of function within the Church (scholar-pastoral theologian-pastor-laity) to be taken as seriously as St. Paul took it; to see the fundamental relationships involved while granting equality of value to each separate sphere. This would at least help to rid us of the current idolatry of "scholarship"—a heresy held by everyone except the genuine scholar—and it might diminish the academic rat-race which is every bit as vicious as the commercial kind. I think it was Professor C. D. Broard who once described the Ph.D. system as that wherein those qualified to do research spent their time supervising those who never would be qualified to do research. Whatever the truth of this aphorism, there is no doubt that our modern divinity faculties swarm with research students the results of whose studies will never be published and in many cases will never be read. I hopefully suggest that they would be better employed doing pastoral theology, regarded as an equal but separate discipline from "scholarship". The results of such studies, demanding every bit as much intellectual application plus spiritual and imaginative insight, would I believe stand up better to the essential qualification for any worthy thesis: that of original thought. True pastoral theology would also dispose of that other bugbear of any Ph.D. in divinity—tacitly accepted but conveniently forgotten—that any really original contribution to doctrinal studies is almost bound, by definition, to be heretical. If the faith was once delivered to the saints, it is difficult to be academically original about it, but its pastoral application from society to society and age to age offers unlimited opportunities for prophetic insight.

The time is opportune for this change of outlook because, for reasons to be considered presently, pastoral theology offers a much wider scope for serious thought and study than ever before. The past tradition—from the *Pastoral Care* of St. Gregory the Great to the pastoral charges of Hensley Henson—has been generally restricted to the more obvious aspects of the "work of a clergyman". Today, theological specialisation, educational, sociological, and ecclesiatical trends, and new experiments in liturgy and spirituality, all offer the coming pastoral theologian far greater scope than the old pastoralia—"what a clergyman ought to do" kind of thing. If specialisation itself demands a corresponding group of pastoral theologians, many a promising young student could well be invited to make a bold decision. If he feels, both intellectually and vocationally, that he might attain to the ranks of first-class scholarship, making genuinely new and original contributions to his subject, all well and good. Otherwise his choice is that between a third-rate scholar *or* a first-rate pastoral theologian. The one adds to the knowledge of his subject, the other fully digests this new knowledge and, by insight, prayer and spiritual imagination, interprets its results to the pastor. It will be argued at this point, especially by the pastor understandably disgruntled by the apparent sterility of academic debate, that the scholarly games now being played never produce results, only a jumble of conflicting theories. But this is a naïve judgement that assumes all theology to be *straight* dogma. We should remember with St. Anselm that theology is not geometry, there can never be a neat Q.E.D. to our quest for the truth about God. But the quest for the knowledge of God is itself venturesome prayer in which, ideally at any rate, a slowly increasing knowledge of God issues not only in theological propositions but in an increased love of God.

Even if there is some excuse for a little pastoral impatience at this lack of results from modern research, there are, nevertheless, clear trends which supply ample material for pastoral theology. To take an example from current biblical studies: whatever the conflicts and however long the experts continue to argue and counter-argue, there is the movement usually called the "new quest for the historical Jesus". It would take no mean student of biblical theology to follow and unravel all that is being said on this one topic, whether or not he can add to the academic controversy itself. But the trend itself is pregnant with practical questions: what does the Christian mean, and what does he experience, by his living faith in the eucharistic "real presence"? What does it mean, if you like how does it feel, to be "in Christ"? How, in prayer, and then inevitably in life, does the sacred humanity of Jesus Christ manifest itself? What does the New Testament say about this and how is the gospel to be approached? All these questions are pastoral-theological ones, and answers to them depend directly on the "quest for the historical Jesus". The man who answers them would have to be a student of considerable learning, competent to follow the trends as well as gifted with a prophetic insight into their practical significance. But he probably would not be a "scholar" in the modern academic sense. Following Karl Rahner, my plea is first that this type of pastoral theological study be embraced by far more competent and mature men, and secondly that these studies be given a recognised status.

A further need arises from the fact that if theology moves and develops with specialised studies it must move *from* a previously held position; tradition is a living stream of unfolding insight, a crystallisation of the experience of the living Church. A student of any specialised branch of theology today, be he academic or pastoral, cannot start from the specialised studies themselves. Yet he must know something of the background and historical development of his subject. With the expansion of modern knowledge this could lead to an infinite regression of preliminary studies: ten or more years of background work before the subject in hand is arrived at. Here is work for a group of pastoral-historians: what are the general trends over, say, two centuries in biblical theology, philosophy of religion, dogmatics, spirituality? The writings resulting from these questions would be not "scholarly" but "popular", or pastoral, or even "potted". But to deride such work is not only intellectual snobbery but a blindness to the integrated theological activity of the whole Church of God. Those of us who read and write theology, of whatever sort, need the humility to see that if scholar-pastoral theologian-pastor-people is the normal order of creative thought, then the order of religious value is the reverse. The ultimate end of all theology, of all teaching, writing and research, is not assessed in degrees and laudatory book-reviews but in the more fruitful confrontation of Christian people with Jesus Christ. That is the existential reality, and that is where we came in.

I reiterate, however, that unless we are to sink into sentimentality the genuine work of both scholar and

D

pastoral theologian is absolutely essential to further this end. It is heartening to note that this kind of pastoral or "potted" study is today being produced, but it is being done on the side, so to speak, by the distinguished scholar of pastoral concern. That such exist in growing numbers is one of the healthiest trends in the modern situation. All praise—to give but a few examples—to John Macquarrie for *Twentieth Century Religious Thought*, R. H. Fuller for *The New Testament in Current Study*, J. Jeremias for *The Central Message of The New Testament*, and I. T. Ramsey for *Christian Discourse*. But we need far more of this kind of writing, and—if the question is not impertinent —is not this the kind of work that the students of international scholars rather than those scholars themselves, should be encouraged to pursue? I think St. Paul suggests that they should: in so doing they would release their professors for the researches only they can do, while if they scorn such popular writing and try to become professorial scholars, the vast majority will fail to produce anything. We must recognise that the only valid motive for any kind of theological endeavour is the pursuance of a vocation in the service of the Church of God.

Once pastoral theology as a disciplined type and method of research is recognised, these possibilities become unlimited. Personally, to give one more example, I believe there must be a serious reappraisal of traditional moral theology. On the other hand I do not find anything but scholasticism and Caroline teaching as possible springboards for such studies, and one cannot evade the laborious reading of these authorities by inventing some superficiality called "pastoral ethics". A tremendous amount of modern thought on morals fails completely by attacking the "traditional position" or "Thomism" or "scholasticism" without really understanding what these things are. We cannot all be Thomists in the scholarly, specialised sense, just because we want to study moral theology; that starts another infinite regression in specialisation. But the Thomist pastoral theologian could well come to our aid, so could the Caroline pastoral theologian and the psychology of religion pastoral theologian.

We are by no means at the end of the modern road. At its optimistic best the position now reached means that we have regained the fullest interpretation of pastoral theology based upon a proper co-operation between those of various gifts within the totality of the body of Christ. We are still thinking of pastoral theology of the old type which makes the assumptions that are no longer valid: the first is that we live in a cultural environment that can broadly be defined by the blanket word "Christendom"; the second maintains a far too simple relationship between "pastor" and "people".

"Christendom" generally means that position wherein the Christian gospel is recognised as the basis of civilisation and learning. No doubt there have been many periods in history when agnosticism or ignorance were as prevalent as they are today, or when the Church was opposed and persecuted. Nevertheless modern notions of "secularity", wherein other secular sources of value are recognised by the Church as well as by society at large, presents a new situation. For the first time we have to consider a working relationship with the secular which is not simply opposition, and the adjective "Christian" may properly be applied to a new range of studies: sociology, psychology political theory, education and so on. And the word "Christian" has to be expanded into a study of subtle relationships which mean more than merely "based on Christian principles". Here it must suffice to point out that the meaning and scope of genuine pastoral theology is thereby widened and deepened.

Spirituality, that is the total life outlook of Christian

societies and individuals based on attitudes of prayer, has alternated throughout history between the speculative and affective emphases: roughly between the intellectual and rational on the one hand and the intuitive and emotional on the other. These emphases have an approximate correspondence with individual responsibility and authoritarian clericalism. In either case the "pastor" is more or less synonymous with "priest" and his guidance consists largely in preaching, exhortation, and the exposition of moral principles. These emphases and relations have been expressed from time to time and place to place in an infinite variety, yet today's combination of intellectual sophistication and ecclesiastical freedom amounts to a new situation. It is no longer valid to assume that the pastor, in the real sense of one deeply concerned for, and equipped to guide, his fellow Christians, is necessarily an ordained minister of the Church. Neither is it now possible to think of the "laity" as some kind of homogeneous group: we have reached the potentially glorious stage where the shepherd, like the Good Shepherd, *must* (not should) "know his sheep" with the deepest spiritual intimacy. This new situation is to be welcomed by any but the most reactionary clericalist, but it creates new problems and demands new adventures in pastoral theology. Anglicanism boasts a group of lay-scholars of the first order, which follows naturally from our seventeenth-century tradition, but the majority of our responsible lay people are not specialist scholars. They are, or should become, pastoral theologians, or pastors, or both: the field of pastoral theological studies has not only widened beyond recognition but it has also discovered a large new audience. This again underlines the need for a clearly defined relationship between scholarship and pastoral theology; both recognised as of equal value, related yet distinct in discipline and approach.

The only satisfactory way to explain this relationship is to *do* some pastoral theology and see how it works, an experiment with which we shall be concerned presently. Meanwhile it must suffice to mention the fundamental differences between the two disciplines.

First, scholarship starts with original sources, with documents and manuscripts, and examines them in minute detail in order to draw out new truth and substantiate hypotheses. It looks *forward* to fresh discovery, and having found it the immediate job is done. If the scholar in question happens to be pastorally-minded he might look back at his work and ask himself if it bears any relevance to practical religion, but this is an optional extra and his work is complete without it: having discovered a new drug the research medico is entitled to a game of golf, he should not be expected to manufacture the pills.

Pastoral theology, on the other hand, starts with pastoral problems within the existential situation, and looks *back* over the widest possible range of historical theology in the hope of lighting upon some doctrine, some doctor, father, saint, that will throw light on the problem and initiate a train of thought which tries to solve it. So wide a range means comparatively shallow knowledge, learned secondhand from commentaries. Since he is dealing with current problems he will obviously include contemporary theology in his wide purview. But, unless he is going to get bogged down in specialised scholarship himself, he may well need the services of our pastoral-biblical, pastoral-dogmatic, pastoral-philosophic theologians to help him to use this new work.

Now it will immediately be apparent that the two disciplines not only start from opposite ends but that pastoral theology comprises a process upon which scholars are wont to pour their most withering scorn. Confronted with a living problem in a concrete situation, the competent pastoral theologian is bound to begin with some personal, even emotional bias towards a solution. He will then look back at historical theology in the hope of finding texts and writings to support it, and this, to the scholar, is the unforgivable sin: the quarrying of proof-texts to prop up a pre-elected prejudice. I maintain, however, that if this is admittedly bad scholarship there is still no reason why it should not be good pastoral theology. That the Association footballer is not allowed to handle the ball does not make Rugby football disreputable: we are playing a different game. The pastoral theological process, moreover, has its own discipline of a frighteningly rigid kind. The true pastoral theologian is sufficiently humble to *distrust* his initial bias or postulated solution that he purposefully seeks the wider experience of the Church's doctrine to test it. If his view can be honestly supported, well and good; if not he must firmly reject it and start again. So to stretch texts and misinterpret books in order to cling to one's point at all costs is unforgivable bigotry; it is not pastoral theology! The pastoral theologian is also dealing with doctrine which must *immediately* affect the lives of Christian people; a far more onerous responsibility than the scholar has to bear. The *direct* leading astray of a brother in Christ through false interpretation is a horror against which the most devastating book review fades into triviality.

Secondly, scholarship is largely analytic; pastoral theology is synthetic. The one concentrates all attention upon a single aspect or strand of theology even if the total theological picture is vaguely seen in the background. The other concentrates on the whole background panorama paying relatively little attention to detail. The former is like the painter of a Dutch miniature, concentrating on every minute detail in disciplined order; the latter is content with a broad landscape like a huge canvas by a

French impressionist. The first is qualified by intense discipline, unending patience, technical skill, detailed knowledge; the second is more intuitive, more imaginative, more experimentally.

Forgive a further analogy. In the solution of a crime there are two ways of looking for clues. There is the painstaking routine search of the professional police where a room or area is divided into small sections, each assigned to an officer who goes over the ground with a toothcomb. He is concerned with his own special area, nobody else's, and when all is done every shred of possible evidence is produced, put together and a theory propounded and followed up. Then there is the search of the intuitive but learned and experienced detective (perhaps existing in the pages of fiction more often than in real life) whose method is to take in a sweeping view of the whole scene. He notices not so much isolated clues but suggestive hints made possible by his wide knowledge of the whole case: the window is fastened when it should be open; the books are clean when they should be dusty; the flower vase has been knocked over that way, should it not have fallen this way? The point is that no solution to the crime is likely until both of these methods are combined. The most brilliant detective (even of fiction) is unlikely to get far without the clues only discoverable by professional— "scholarly"—searching. On the other hand these clues are valueless until someone fits them together and gives them meaning, and this is only possible by a detective of the "pastoral theological" kind: one who is looking at the total picture with a synthesis of knowledge and intuition. It is perhaps not without significance that, in detective fiction, the amateur who evades the plodding routine and breaks most of the rules is not too highly regarded by the professional police. Conversely, he looks on them as dull-witted plodders. And it is even more significant that

despite this rivalry, they usually get on pretty well together and finally recognise their interdependence:
were theology in so happy a state!

The third distinction concerns the immediate end-
product and its presentation. The end-product of scholarship is not necessarily (in fact very rarely) a nice neat
system of new knowledge rounded off with a final Q.E.D.
It is nevertheless a body of knowledge of some kind, a
convincing hypothesis which is intellectually satisfying.
The end-product of pastoral theology, on the other hand,
must be closely related to prayer; it is to inspire meditative or contemplative response to grace in a given
situation, or to be incorporated into a working system of
spirituality. In which case some tiny insight into a revealed mystery, some poetic image, or myth, or seeming
contradiction, may be more fruitful than a neat and tidy
dogma. This is St. Anselm's *credo ut intellegam*: the adventurous quest of faith in response to the love of God which,
though grounded in dogma, is enlightened by speculation
and by theological paradox.

Scholarship is usually presented in logical, documented,
and prosaic form; it must be well reasoned and supported
by authorities. It is to be hoped that pastoral theology
also contains some semblance of reason, logic and authoritarian support, but it may also contain a good deal of
metaphor, parable and analogy. This is why the Bible is
predominantly pastoral theology, the end-products of
which are prayer inspired by spiritual perception and
illumination, as well as straight doctrinal fact. (Perhaps
I should add that this point is made in good faith and not
to excuse my own undisciplined use of analogy!)

If this is a legitimate distinction between scholarship
and pastoral theology, it is nevertheless of interest to the
argument that, in current scholarship, the dividing line
becomes more and more blurred. With its "maps",

"models" and "myths", theological language is rapidly moving away from the old substantive kind of statement. Thus in *Christian Discourse*, I. T. Ramsey can offer some strong criticism against Dr. Hastings Rashdall for belittling the value and theological status of metaphor. The same point is elaborated by E. J. Tinsley in his valuable sixth essay in the symposium *Vindications*. And John McIntyre makes a similar plea for the theological (not only meditative and expository) reinstatement of the category of imagination. (*The Shape of Christology*, pp. 128, 172 ff.) If metaphor and analogy is becoming respectable in theological scholarship, it has always been an essential inspiration to Christian prayer. With some optimism it may be hoped that the two are drawing closer together.

I think it was T. S. Eliot who said something to the effect that an educated man was one who, faced with any idea, was able roughly to plot it on the whole map of human culture of all ages. In this narrower context that exactly describes what I mean by pastoral theology. The pastoral theologian is one who is theologically educated, which is different from being a scholar. He is one who, faced with a pastoral problem, is able roughly to plot it on the map of Christian theology of all ages.

Unless we are to stretch the phrase beyond normal use, it is now necessary to move beyond pastoral theology. The emphasis has to move from group guidance, whether by books or sermons, to the use of theology by individuals in an infinite variety of practical situations. The corporate aspect of prayer, in and of the body of Christ, remains, but as the foundation, not the frustration, of responsible individuality: we have moved from pastoral to *applied* theology.

CHAPTER FOUR

Applied Theology

The movement from scholar to pastor and pastor to people roughly corresponds with the movement from straight theology through pastoral theology to applied theology. It is also a movement from the corporate aspects of doctrine towards individuality. The conclusions of scholarship finally issue in dogma, straight facts which pertain to all Christian people and which influence their lives more or less spontaneously. In these days of unending theological dispute this bland statement may well seem far too simple, and in many ways it is, but it is true historically and it continues to be true to modern scholarly intent: however long the road may be scholarship must look to the hope of dogmatic discovery, to plain truths whether officially promulgated or not.

Pastoral theology issues in explanation and directive to a group of Christians under the care of a pastor, and it has largely consisted in spiritual obligations and moral precepts adapted to the needs of the local group. Such directive, usually disseminated by preaching, varies from the authoritative manual and penitentiary to more thoughtful and responsible guidance, according to the width of the scholar-pastor-people gap in a given situation. Applied theology goes further in emphasising the unique integrity and responsibility of individual Christians, and their need for competent guidance, more exacting for the pastor—whether clerical or lay—than ever before. This is at the heart of the modern pastoral situation, and it may be put in another way, which has clear associations with modern philosophies and with modern social trends. Scholarship-pastoral theology-applied theology is also a movement from intellectualism to existential living. Whatever the devotion and sanctity of individual scholars their work issues in intellectual statements. The pastor, guided by pastoral theology, is concerned with more than this; at least with moral behaviour and ecclesiastical discipline. Applied theology is concerned with nothing less than all the ways and means of Christian living, with an intellectual grasp of doctrine, moral and spiritual discipline, *and* a full development of prayer, which aids and supports a person's total approach to Christ with his whole being. Through the complexities necessitated by modern life, and the controversies which continue after nearly twenty centuries of Christian experience, we are back to the commitment involved in a living confrontation with Jesus Christ.

Once this scheme of things is accepted more light is thrown on some of the shortcomings of current theological thought. The scholar is inclined to see his work either as straight theology, spontaneously meaningful to ordinary Christians, or as a value in its own right of no significance to the Church at large with which he admits little concern. But even the scholar of broader outlook is inclined to stop short at pastoral theology, failing to see the inevitability of the third stage and therefore failing to serve the needs of the modern pastor in his guidance of responsible individuals. Such pastoral writing that we have is designed to serve the preacher and group-pastor but not the deep spiritual understanding needed by the individual guide. Trends in the various departments of theology fall into the first category, pastorally-orientated expositions of modern moral theology fall into the second. Neither goes far enough.

To take a composite example: a scholar may study the implications of the doctrines of sin and grace and produce new insights couched in technical idiom; technical not only in established theological words but also including much of the modern jargon which has grown up around his specialised subject. A pastoral theologian may then absorb this work and decide that it should be made more meaningful to modern man by changing the language. But he still has in mind the "congregation" or some general abstraction like the "ordinary Christian". He has not considered the needs of responsible persons like George, Mary and Henry, or even that a pastor can guide them and that they may be able to guide one another. Once this new pastoral situation is recognised the study of religious language takes on a new significance. In a truly pastoral essay called "Existentialism and the Christian Vocabulary" (*Studies in Christian Existentialism*, part 3, chap. 9) John Macquarrie has thrown much light on the fact "that words like 'grace', 'sin', 'faith' have *for most people* lost the force and freshness which presumably they once possessed" (my italics). Now in the hands of a Christian pastor, or as a discussable subject amongst Christian people, what Macquarrie has to say here could be wonderfully fruitful in assisting a more real, and more worthy confrontation with Christ; his exposition could lead to a healthier sense of penitence and a livelier faith, especially through a more vivid understanding of, and co-operation with, grace. But with respect, I do not think Macquarrie sees his thought in this context and this confuses the issue. "For most people" hints at an assumption, not of advanced personal endeavour but of a vague and general attempt at apologetic and evangelism. Changes in the Christian vocabulary and a study of the reasons

for the change may assist committed Christian persons,
although after the process they may well prefer to retain
the old words. Changing the words might conceivably rid
"most people"—or a few of them—of some blatant
misconceptions about the Christian faith, but it will do no
more than alter their agnostic intellectual knowledge.
There may be something to be said for following Tillich
and calling sin "estrangement", in modern context it
may even be a more accurate word, but it will not make
anyone but the virile Christian more penitent. In the
essay under discussion, Macquarrie has written very
successful pastoral theology but it is most successful in the
hands of the personal spiritual guide, that is as applied
theology. If the ideas of evangelism and apologetic creep
in, the essay loses most of its force and reverts to helping
"most people" to understand, in intellectual terms, what
Christianity means: it reverts from pastoral to straight
theology, or at best to pastoral theology in the group-
preaching, almost the manual-penitentiary, sense. It is
a little ironical that Macquarrie himself would be the
first to insist that if Christianity really stands for anything in the modern world, then nothing less than total
commitment, existential encounter with one's whole
being, living experience of and in Christ, will do.

There are related problems which the concept of applied
theology may help to solve. Macquarrie is doing valuable
service to pastoral theology by harnessing Christian
concepts to existentialism of a sane post-Bultmann type,
but he readily admits that no one philososphy can ever
contain the Christian religion. Applied theology may,
indeed must, make use of many philosophical concepts
irrespective of fashion. Yet in spite of Macquarrie's
philosophical humility the current vogue is towards
existentialist concepts and away from metaphysics and
ontology. Much modern study of Christian doctrine

consists in the attempt to translate substantive credal formulae into terms of existence and relationship. This process could be of use to pastoral and applied theology, but it is tacitly assumed that the traditional formulae are, in themselves, out of date and worthless. This, I suggest, is but a shallow following of fashion which fails to ask *the* existential question: What is this, or any other theology *for*? What is its function?

My own position—and I think Macquarrie would agree with it—is well illustrated by James Barr's treatment of the old Hebraism versus Hellenism controversy. (*Old and New in Interpretation*, pp. 34–64). On the simplest level (and what follows is no doubt a caricature of the position held by serious scholars) it is suggested that the religion of Jesus was Hebraic, living, historical, existential, rather than intellectual and dogmatic. The Hebrew God was known through worship and prayer, he acted in history, he was the God of the living not of the dead. It was the Greeks, aided and abetted by St. Paul, who took all the life out of the thing and coffined it all up in theoretical dogma. With Macquarrie, though in a different context, Barr shatters this sort of theory by a most convincing argument that the living faith required, and took unto itself, not Hebrew or Greek thought, or a complex of the two, but thought forms from many other sources as well. The test was not the fashion of the moment but the service of living religion, the living confrontation with the risen Lord, with pastoral and applied theology.

Modern studies must continue along their specialised course, and new existential interpretations of the ancient formulae could be of much practical use, but I think we still suffer from the dual idolatry of "scholarship" and "fashion". If we ask what the traditional formulae are *for*, if we move from straight theology to pastoral and applied theology and ask what is spiritually useful as well

as what is intellectually satisfying, then modern studies
might receive a new impetus and a more worthy direction.
As an example let us follow out this approach with regard
to Chalcedonian Christology.

The Chalcedonian Definition may be approached in
any of the ways, or uses, of practical theology under consideration. It starts as straight theology, it may become
pastoral, and it can finally be applied. This in itself means
that Chalcedonian Christology may be inadequate; in the
sense that it is couched in unfamiliar terms it may even be
dated, but it cannot be dismissed on the grounds that it is
metaphysical or ontological or "Greek". It is *usable*, and
whatever difficulties it fails to solve, it arose from a
process of thought necessitated not only by intellectual
curiosity but by the most practical needs of the earliest
disciples in confrontation with the risen Christ. Whatever
answers Chalcedon provides, the questions first arose in
the heart of Magdalene: is this man also God whom I
may love and adore? The answer "yes" is straight theology, it solves the immediate problem. Christ is risen and
alive for ever, he is fully human and freely approachable,
he is wholly divine and adorable. To Magdalene and the
holy women, and no doubt to many faithful people today,
all that is straight theology which leads to a certain
activity and a certain outlook once it is accepted in faith.
However substantive the formulation, it is practical
doctrine. Thus the interpretation of doctrine in modern
terms can mean two different things. It can mean trans-
lating an ancient formula into modern terminology, or
expounding old philosophical categories in ways more
congenial to modern thought. *Or* it can mean *using* the
old formulae in modern prayer. Once Chalcedon is
absorbed, that is spiritually understood—when it has
"sunk in"—and when the Christ it described is confronted
in prayer, then Chalcedon *is* relevant to the existential

situation. We are in a present relation with one who is a divine and human nature, inseparable yet unconfused in one person. Similarly when a Christian lives intelligently within the Church's threefold regula the doctrine of the Trinity *is* existential experience, in whatever formula it is expressed. It is never sufficient to modernise doctrine simply for it to be better understood. Conversely, if a doctrine is usable in prayer there is little point in modernising it, unless such a process includes new insights. The point forgotten by the academic philosopher is that a statement may be substantive or existential according to practical context as well as verbal form. "There is a train to London at 2.20" is a "substantial" statement which means little to those who do not wish to go to London. But if a journey to London is imperative it becomes a vital, practical, "existential" statement leading to immediate action. Chalcedon is the same; according to whether or not one desires to confront and enter a dialogue with the risen Christ.

Nevertheless this spontaneous reaction to a dogmatic fact leads to further questions for a speculative mind and to possible dangers for the unsophisticated. Here the pastor, and if need be the pastoral theologian, is required to elaborate by teaching and preaching. It would be wise to explain that confrontation with the risen Christ, in prayer, or recollection, or in the eucharist, was a unique experience in which God must be adored and the sacred humanity freely approached at one and the same time. Christ does not alternate between God and man from time to time, we dare not be over-familiar with the human Jesus on the assumption that sometimes God was not there, or that he was not looking. Neither need our proper and growing awe of God Almighty ever be allowed to degenerate into servile terror, because Jesus remains always our one perfect advocate with the Father. But

Jesus Christ is always wholly divine and wholly man, there is no separation, or confusion, or mixture. That is pastoral theology, and I think it is very much Chalcedonian pastoral theology. It concerns living questions and existential attitudes, but only when it is taught, thought about, accepted and "absorbed". Pastorally interpreted, it is neither dead nor difficult, but it is one stage removed from straight doctrine.

Christian people have unique gifts and unique problems arising from temperament, environment, intelligence and moral perception. Every person finds himself in a constant series of new situations. To one the sacred humanity is an attractive idea, naturally overflowing into affective prayer which in turn overflows into a particular type of Christian outlook. To another the sacred humanity is a stumbling block to a natural sense of awe for God Almighty, or it could be regarded as a necessary part of the creed which alone makes intellectual sense of the doctrine of the Atonement. We are back with all the old divisions of human temperament: the affective and speculative, the intuitive and the intellectual, the mystical and the moral. But all these types of Christian outlook are both right and imperfect: right because Christianity recognises that grace perfects not abstract "nature" but unique individual nature, inadequate because every unequal emphasis risks error and because all facets of both creed and character have some place in Christian living. However the elements vary, the affective, speculative, intuitive, rational, mystical and moral, have their proportionate places in a total Christian experience. Balance is necessary and I suggest that a formula, or map or model, like Chalcedon, remains an essentially practical guide in guarding against error and developing the central hub of total response. Modern man is at one with first-century man in wanting guidance as to who and what Jesus is, substantially, rationally and

E

metaphysically, in order to know how to respond in existential confrontation with him. As Barr demonstrates, the old "Hebrew-Greek" edges become blurred, but in practical affairs this means that the "Greek" formula must be individually applied to every existential situation.

New Christological thought, interpreted in terms of living relationship between the divine and human natures rather than in terms of Greek metaphysics, may give impetus to applied theology as well as making up for some of the admitted inadequacies of Chalcedon. Indeed such a new Christology is required by the change of emphasis in spiritual theology wherein the manifestation of Christ is sought more in his indwelling of human persons than in imaginative pictures or symbolic images: "Christ in people" *versus* the "historical Jesus". If we accept applied, or ascetical, theology as the end-product of pastoral thought, then Chalcedon has much value still. If it is inadequate this is because there have been changes and developments in spirituality not because Chalcedon is static, or substantive, or "Greek". But as so often happens in pastoral theology, "new" thought turns out to be a rediscovery of what has long been forgotten. In *The Shape of Christology* (pp. 99–101), John McIntyre does us pastoral service by unearthing—for me at any rate—the Chalcedonian interpretation of Ephraim of Antioch. The relevant twist is, to quote McIntyre: "But what I consider to be his originality emerges when he tries to explain the 'two natures in the union which is according to *hypostasis*' by saying that while the two natures as such are not confused or compounded one with the other, the two *hypostases* are. Accordingly the *hypostasis* of Jesus Christ is a fusion of the human and divine *hypostasis*: it is *synthetos hē hypostasis*." The result of this interpretation is to rid Chalcedon of its implied "impersonal" view of the sacred humanity: "the *logos* took not only *humanitas* but *homo*."

McIntyre goes on to develop this implication in terms of soteriology, which is legitimate, but is not its real significance to be seen in prayer? And is not this prayer a necessary step from doctrine to soteriological influence in life? The practical fact is that one cannot hold colloquy with *humanitas*, only with *homo*. This shows up the *living* inadequacy of Chalcedon, and here it is provided for. I am not concerned either to substantiate or to condemn Chalcedon: only to suggest that its study is still usable as a source of pastoral theology, and that it is prayer which makes it usable.

As well as rendering all existing doctrine of practical use to Christian life, applied theology may well rebound to the stimulation of fresh theological thought. The pastoral recognition of applied theology ought to inspire the scholar by bringing him more fully into the redemptive life of the modern Church. However erudite his findings, he need no longer retire to some scholarly enclave and feel useless. For if pastoral and applied theology are recognised, they will not only inspire the modern scholar but will also liberate scholarship from the bonds of fashion. Within this context the reinterpretation of doctrine in existentialist terms has an obvious place, but so have ecclesiastical history and patristic studies. Coupled with applied theology, these are no longer sterile and old-fashioned but of current significance. It is not so much a question of studying the Fathers to see if their doctrine still has any relevance, still less of stretching and straining texts to make them appear relevant. The need is for scholars to expound and clarify patristic teaching so that pastoral theologians may recognise its relevance when it does in fact impinge on a concrete situation.

To give proper consideration to the current pastoral facts two further points must be made. The first is that, even within the domestic ethos of the Anglican pastoral tradition, modern spiritual theology reacts strongly against the dangers of "over-direction". This is not only a healthy reaction against clerical authoritarianism but a more positive move towards individual responsibility. On the other hand the pastoral emphasis is equally strong on the need for deep personal relationships in Christian living while our recent preoccupation with the parish group is diminishing. This adds up to a series of deep loving relationships within the body of Christ but with a minimum of formal direction.

Secondly, spiritual guidance by applied theology is rapidly ceasing to be a clerical preserve and is becoming one of the rightly central aspects of the lay-apostolate. Together the two points demand more and more pastoral theology in published form and should give another impetus to its production. With St. Bernard I do not believe that serious Christian life can be entirely guided by books, the need for personal encounter and guidance will always remain, yet the quest for a creative minimum of formal direction is, I am sure, a healthy sign. The guidance necessary for Christian development will, therefore, swing more and more towards books and informal intercourse between Christians whether clerical or lay. The professional pastor's job becomes, on the one hand more theological, for he has to watch over his flock from the viewpoint of applied theology, and on the other hand more deeply personal both in his relations with those who guide others and with those he guides himself.

To do ustice to modern thought, the rendering of dogma into pastoral doctrine, and pastoral theology into applied theology, is a process more than a merely intellectual exercise. It demands human understanding, intuitive insights and spiritual perception as well as learning, and the fact that I couple applied with what is more technically called ascetical theology points clearly to prayer as mediator within the total theological scheme. It is mediator between the straight-pastoral-applied complex and also between any of these and Christian action. Rather than a glibly pious idea, the "centrality of prayer" has become both the theological and practical key to Christian life. There have been times when reason was paramount in the Church's life: we must follow reason right to the end. At other times conscience ruled: we must follow conscience right to the end. The modern fashion is to give priority to love: we must in all things follow love right to the end. That is orthodox and biblical enough, but only when love is interpreted in orthodox and biblical fashion: as a total commitment to Christ and neighbour with the totality of one's being, which includes rather than diminishes the demands of reason and conscience. Modern thought and orthodoxy thus become united: not just reason, or conscience, or even love, but nothing less than the integrity of the whole complex human being may validly be followed right to the end. And this means, in technical terms, "spirituality", for only prayer as response to Christ is able to grapple with an existential confrontation. Only prayer understood as this total response, recapitulating the mind, body, intuitive insights, human understanding and all the rest, can mediate between theology and the wholeness of Christian life. This central fact must, then, be demonstrated, elaborated, and finally examined in terms of the practical situation.

CHAPTER FIVE

The Centrality of Prayer

Without the mediation of prayer, all theology except *straight* dogma becomes sterile, and even dogma tends to become assented to without impingement upon practical life. Conversely, prayer, in the sense of the "absorption" of doctrine, or even of speculation, is able to fertilise the most recondite learning and to produce pastoral and ascetical theology. If the modern scholar seldom gets beyond the conception of straight doctrine, however much he tries to interpret it in terms intelligible to modern people, he seems singularly inept at producing it, and this rebounds to the bewilderment, not to say frustration, of the new theology-reading public. The modern Christian, cleric or lay, is only baffled and his faith is possibly harmed, by his attempt to unravel the contradictions and controversies of the specialists. But the mistake is two-sided: the scholar sees no further than his own specialised field, while the non-specialist looks at theology solely for intellectual satisfaction. He expects speculative theology to behave like geometry with a neat Q.E.D. at the end of every book. This is as ingenuous as those who reject the Bible because it "contradicts itself": Paul says we are justified by faith, James that we are justified by works—so why bother? Yet, spiritually discerned, "absorbed" by prayer, meditated upon in response to the Spirit, it is precisely the paradoxes, speculations, myths, parables and miracles that give the Bible meaning to practical faith. And I believe this is the key to all other theology as well; it is a continuous quest for the knowledge of God, a quest which will never be completed in this life but which, little by little, inspires and unfolds to lead the Christian to greater spiritual discernment and to increase in the love of God. This is the secret of St. Anselm, who had little interest in "proving the existence of God" to the agnostic or in explaining the doctrine of the Atonement by way of apologetic or evangelism. His faith demanded understanding in order that his faith should expand and manifest itself more fully. I repeat the plea made elsewhere (*English Spirituality*, chap. 14, ii, pp. 157–63) that *Proslogium* and *Cur Deus Homo*? be removed from the "philosophy of religion" and "dogmatic" shelves and placed together under "devotion".

This approach is particularly important, and especially apposite, to the theological mood of today; firstly from the non-specialist pastoral point of view and secondly from that of current scholarship. To the ordinary, non-specialist Christian, modern theological controversy is necessarily bewildering and often disturbing. One of the commonest criticisms brought against Bishop Robinson is that *Honest to God* "disturbs the faithful" but this is a manifestation of the over-intellectual "Q.E.D" approach. Robinson and van Buren disturb those who are content to "hold" dogmatic statements but not, I think, those whose Christian lives are ruled by an Anselmic struggle, quest or faith-venture into the mysteries of God by prayer. The only prayerful people who are likely to be disturbed by new theological speculation are those whose orthodoxy is in danger of formalism. Speculative theology, in other words, disturbs those who have got themselves into one or another kind of rut: such disturbance is no bad thing. But if those in the intellectual rut are shaken out against their will, those in the prayer rut are invited to jump out with renewed zeal.

From the position of modern scholarship the centrality of prayer is even more far-reaching. Spoken at the start of a lecture or address, this very phrase, "the centrality of prayer", is apt to be received by a series of devout nods as a piece of piety which nobody is prepared to argue about—or bother about. Yet the total approach to modern thought, carried over into theological studies, demands that the phrase be taken seriously.

In this wide, deep sense, prayer is a total experience of all things in Christ. It is an habitual consideration of people and things through the Incarnation which gradually gives a new dimension to experience and to learning: an added discernment of truth, a contemplative perception of the unseen source of life.

The breakdown of Christendom and the emergence and acceptance of the secular has driven the Church to some healthy reappraisal of her place within the total culture. However influential Chritianity has been in learning, art, medicine, drama, architecture and law, we now know and admit that these things can get on perfectly well without it. Yet it is equally true that no total civilisation, in East or West, Christian or pagan, has ever arisen and survived without the contemplative element. "Contemplatives" writes Hans Urs von Balthasar "are like great subterreanean rivers, which, on occasion, break out into springs at unexpected points, or reveal their presence only by the plants they feed from below". (*Prayer*, p. 73.) It is true that secular culture, in its manifold departments, can get on well enough without religion, and it is childish to go on pretending that it cannot. Yet the dry bones of a total civilisation still need contemplative fertilisation; the catalyst of prayer applies to the departments of a pluralist culture as it does to theology itself.

Prayer is still central to human existence, and theology is essential to prayer. Within society as a whole, it is this dimension that the Church can give, and her greatest sin against her Lord and against creation is failure to give it: to poke around the fringes of the secular to the neglect of her unique contribution. It is in this context that we should consider the centrality of prayer to modern theology itself; here it must suffice to look briefly at three specialised subjects: biblical studies, religious philosophy, and moral theology. One of the most obvious trends in current spiritual theology is a return to the Bible as both source of serious prayer and as foundation for renewed ascetical theology. It is significant that the great three-volume work of Père Pourrat, *Christian Spirituality*, first published in 1920, starts with the briefest introductory chapter on "the ascetic teaching of Jesus and the Apostles". Louis Bouyer's replacement of this work *A History of Christian Spirituality*, 1960, begins with a lengthy chapter on Old Testament spirituality and continues with six further chapters—164 pages in all—on the spiritual theology of the New Testament. It should be understood, however, that this is no isolated new fashion in spiritual theology but a logical corollary to the current approach to biblical theology itself.

In *An Introduction to the Theology of the New Testament*, Dr. Alan Richardson explains that "New Testament Theology" is an approach to the Bible through the eyes of the Apostolic Church, assumed to be possessed of a clear theological conviction of its own. The New Testament has long ceased to be regarded as a set of autonomous historical documents, or as a series of divine propositions, or as a biography of Jesus of Nazareth. It is rather the record of the confrontation between Jesus Christ and the twelve, the record of the Early Church's spiritual experience. And spiritual experience is notoriously difficult to write down in clear logical terms. The New Testament, therefore, is forced to speak in various languages, in terms of law and of love; of doctrinal fact, pastoral directive and faith-venture; by parable, myth, symbol and analogy. As Dr. Richardson continues to point out, such records of spiritual experience cannot adequately be expounded in terms of logic, intellectual proposition or the historically objective. They demand of scholars things like "insight", "perception", and "faith". Richardson speaks of a "flash of insight" and is even bold enough to use the word "hunch" in this context: "New Testament theology . . . cannot 'prove' historical (or theological) hypotheses, but it can test them . . . A proper understanding of Christian origins or of New Testament history is possible only through the insight of Christian faith . . . New Testament theology partakes of the character of *fides quaerens intellectum*" (op. cit. pp. 13–14.) All this means that modern biblical scholarship takes on much of the character of what used to be called "intellectual meditation" in its highest sense; the disciplined synthesis of speculative thought with affective insight, faith in search of understanding the mind of God. So "biblical scholarship" and the "spirituality of the Bible" come to much the same thing; modern words may look difficult and obscure to the ordinary man, yet they are more potentially pastoral than ever before: "New Testament theology is not something which can be left by the preachers and teachers of the churches to specialists in universities and seminaries: it concerns the Sunday sermon, the Bible class, the catechism, and indeed the whole of the life of the local Church." Two riders follow: the admission that modern biblical studies *are* specialised creates a need for adaptation in pastoral and ascetical terms, and such adaptation must take on the character of biblical studies themselves—the return to faith, insight, discernment, and prayer rather than propositional statements. Through pastoral and ascetical interpretation, scholarship returns to the living Church as existential experience.

In my student days there was a professor of biblical theology who achieved fame in his chosen field as well as a certain notoriety for never going to church if he could possibly help it. I do not think that such a situation is any longer possible, a man who was unconcerned about prayer and worship could not now be a biblical scholar at all. He could study texts and manuscripts, he could undertake a type of historical research, but he could not pursue biblical theology with its spiritually discerned insights, faith, and even hunches.

The centrality of prayer has recently become a leading factor in modern moral theology. On an everyday level, "modern" morality favours "situation ethics" set against categorical "blanket judgements", erroneously supposed to be characteristic of "traditional" Christian moral theology. This extremely naïve view discounts the whole tradition of Christian casuistry which goes back at least to the decision of Mattathias to fight if attacked on the Sabbath (I Macc. 2. 41). The new foe (or the old bogey) is, of course, "legalism", a word which is wont to be used in pastoral contexts with more emotion than precision. Strictly, a "legalist" moral system is one built upon the concept of law as its foundation, a non-legalist system is one built upon some other foundation, but this does not necessarily mean the total rejection of law, still less does it imply a supposed conflict between law and love. Thus a modern moralist of impeccable orthodoxy writes: "Such terms (*salvation*, *commandment* and *law*) and their concepts will retain their full value. However, none of them is the focal centre of Catholic moral teaching." (Bernard Häring, *The Law of Christ*, vol. I, p. 46.) If modern moral thought is anti-legalist in the strict sense—discounting the extreme antinomian wing—of rejecting law as the *foundation* of a moral system, its more common weakness is that love simply cannot form a satisfactory substitute: love may, indeed it must, be the guide and end-product of Christian morals, but it cannot also be their *foundation*. Häring continues: "To our mind the term *responsibility* understood in its religious sense is the more apt." Law thus becomes much what it was to St. Paul—"our schoolmaster to bring us to Christ"—or in Häring's phrase "The law is the warning which safeguards liberty." (*op. cit.* p. 103.)

Häring's concept of *responsibility*, however, "understood in its religious sense" means to understand it in a strikingly literal sense: it is the *ability* to make a *response* which implies dialogue, and in Christian terms, a responsible dialogue with Christ. Church history shows up a distressing series of divorces and remarriages between morals and ascetics, but in the best and most responsible modern thought these are more closely wedded than ever before. Modern moral doctrine begins, not with law and certainly not with love, but with response to the prevenient love of Christ, and this is not only a sound moral theological principle but an attractive one to the modern mind. The trouble with traditional casuistry is that, while attempting to combat "blanket" legalism, it is ever in danger of degenerating into a more sophisticated legalism of its own. "Situation ethics", when rid of blatant antinomianism, imply a responsible spontaneity of moral judgement, a freedom in which the whole personality reacts to an existential situation. Casuistry is still largely rational, the careful working out of an approach to moral problems; "situation ethics" gives a proper value to intuition and emotion, in fact to full human integrity. This sounds attractive, but if we are speaking within a Christian context, it presupposes something even more difficult to acquire than the traditional "trained conscience"; nothing less in fact than a continuous recollected response to Jesus Christ, which is the outcome only of a regular and disciplined life of prayer. We are back, though in a refreshing new guise, to the old tenet that all moral theology begins and ends with the acquisition and preservation of sanctifying grace. So to start any moral discussion with something other than prayer as response to grace is not only untheological but out of date. To grant love precedence over law is in tune with every responsible moral theological trend, but to divorce love from theology applied to personal prayer is also outmoded.

It is many centuries since professional philosophy has been so closely related with the outlook of ordinary people as it is today, and two aspects of this philosophy support biblical and moral theology in giving a new centrality to prayer. "Existentialism" has obvious roots in a human reaction to the catastrophic events of this century, and it is significant that it is to a large extent expressed in plays, novels and poetry rather than in scholarly argument: so was the teaching of Jesus. This pinpoints the second aspect of philosophy which concerns us here: the problem of religious language.

Current philosophical emphases—which, be it remembered, have the closest relations with the modern outlook of ordinary people—are away from philosophies of substance and being towards those of existence, experience and activity. The concern is not with what a thing *is* but with what it *does* and what it is *for*. This in itself should have overwhelming repercussions in theological studies of every kind, for however necessary metaphysical and ontological statements of dogma may be, they can no longer merely be "believed in" or "held". They must be translated into usable terms of relationships, of pastoral and applied doctrine, while in practice, prayer remains the essential translator. If the key terms of existentialist thought—"present concrete experience", "commitment", "authentic existence", and so on—are given a Christian interpretation, then we are back with a confrontation and continuing relationship with Jesus Christ: that is with prayer. Existential experience, moreover, pertains to the total man; it is a return to the biblical doctrine of the absolute unity of the individual person, and only prayer is sufficient to co-ordinate and guide all the various psychological and emotional elements in a complete person. This gives a new twist to practically all contemporary thought about pastoral theology. The "problem of communication" must start with prayer; "religious education" is meaningless without it; "preaching" presupposes it; and we must seriously consider whether the old distinctions like "sins of the flesh" and "sins of the spirit", or "mental" and "contemplative" prayer, are any longer valid.

So with the question of religious language. The logical positivists must be right in asserting that if the word "God" by definition means a supreme, omnipotent, omniscient, ultimately incomprehensible being, or even simply a unique being, then the word is logically meaningless. The question is no longer whether statements like "God exists" or "God is love" are right or wrong but whether they have any intelligible meaning at all. And the answer must be that theological statements cannot be confined to the logical. So religious language, like biblical and existential language, has to find expression in parable, poetry and analogy. And the understanding of these demand the spiritual qualities of perception, insight, intuition and faith which are nurtured by prayer.

In *Christian Discourse*, Professor I. T. Ramsey writes: "Christian conviction arises when and only when a cosmic disclosure occurs for us around some of the historical events which form part of the Christian dispensation—only when around these events something breaks in on us, only when the eye for scientific and historical detail is fulfilled in the eye of faith." (p. 23.) To Ramsey, our knowledge of God ultimately depends on these qualities we have been considering: a deepening insight, a "vision", a "cosmic disclosure". This is why Jesus spoke in parables. This faith, moreover, this insight and disclosure, is a progressive factor which grows and deepens as Christians mature, and it sounds to me very closely linked with contemplative prayer.

Bishop Ramsey continues thus: "The question which plagues us is: granting historical uncertainties, on what condition is such Christian conviction reasonable?" Or to broaden the question: if all theology is at bottom analogical, which formula, theory, credal statement, "model", is it reasonable to accept? Evoking Bishop Butler, Ramsey suggests that the "reasonable" is the "probable", for "probability is the guide of life." But there is a further test: "if we have 'seen' with the eye of faith, it must presumably have some particular bearing on our behaviour, so that we may expect there to be some relevant feature of that behaviour to which we may significantly point." Bishop Ramsey is writing philosophy, not ascetical theology, but is not this something like the hoary old error (or evasion, or inadequacy) which jumps straight from faith to works without the mediation of grace through prayer? Is not prayer itself another, and more workable test for the reasonableness of doctrinal models and analogies? If these are contemplated and prove capable of being "absorbed", or if on meditation they yield more and more progressive insight or disclosure, are they not reasonable? In fact, to faith, are they not "right"?

Further, Ramsey makes much of the verb "to see', especially with regard to the resurrection stories (John 20. 5) and the following story of the doubts of St. Thomas. This is an elaboration of F. C. Copleston's fundamental distinction between "seeing" and "noticing" (*Contemporary Philosophy*, chap. 6), and I would suggest that if there is a progression from casually noticing to seeing in detail; from, in Ramsey's terms, "the glancing eye to the eye of faith"; from glancing at, to seeing, to observing, to understanding, to entering deeply into, then the operative process itself is contemplative prayer.

All this has the deepest implications for theological usage and particularly for pastoral practice. It is commonly assumed, for example, that evangelistic and liturgical preaching are but two types of the same thing, but is this still valid? The liturgical proclamation of the gospel to the believing Church, as part of the worship of God known by revelation and in faith, is an intelligible act. But has an intellectual discourse about "God" to an agnostic audience any validity at all? Is not the whole process of communication irrevocably cut off by an iron curtain of logic? The answer is that if we are still trying to "prove" the existence of God, or to argue the unbeliever into faith, the position is impossible. But this need not be the case: the Spirit may act through the preacher but then we are back to prayer as the literal first need. It may well prove that the modern first step in making the Bible and the creeds not intelligible but *usable* to the modern congregation, is to introduce it to the various types of theological language instead of trying to translate theology into "ordinary" language.

CHAPTER SIX

Prayer as Interpreter of Theology

The confrontation of the disciple, original or contemporary, with Jesus Christ is prayer. Reflection upon the problems raised by such confrontation issues in theology, which turns back to prayer. There is the fundamental cycle: prayer-theology-prayer. Prayer, therefore, develops as the experience of the Church unfolds, so in speaking of "modern" prayer I am thinking in terms of the continuance of a tradition, not of the breach with tradition. It is indeed my hope to show that theology remains the raw material—the stuff to be *used*—in the formulation of "modern" prayer.

Despite a necessary over-simplification, the current trend may be expressed as a movement away from intellectualism towards a total, more fully human experience; from knowledge to intuition; or in more philosophical terms from substance to existence. In spite of appearances, or of popular opinion, I think there is a reaction against the scientific as an explanation of life. To the modern mind a botanical description of a rose is not a rose any more than a creed is religion. A hundred years ago a man who said that he was "religious but had no use for dogma" would be regarded as irresponsible, as making an excuse for laxity in religious observance. Today this statement should be taken more seriously, and if it were slightly changed into "I am religious but I have no use

F

for *mere* dogma", then I think we should have a valid expression of a truly religious modern mind. Dogma has to show that it can be used and that its use makes practical sense in human experience. And prayer is the necessary catalyst which alone can translate doctrine, and perhaps substantive statements from philosophy, science, psychology and other things as well, into living experience and value. But plainly "prayer" in this sense is a larger thing altogether than the pious appendage to religion that it has regrettably become. How, then, can we describe it?

Karl Rahner defines man as "the being of receptive spirituality standing in freedom before God, who is free in regard to a possible revelation: a revelation which, if it occurs, takes on the form of a word spoken in man's history" (*Horer des Wortes*, p. 209). This sort of experience ("prayer") means the fullest insight, the richest interpretation of human experience because it claims his whole being and his most complete sensitivity. It is I. T. Ramsey's "cosmic disclosure".

This, I believe, is the true aspiration of modern people, religious or otherwise. On the surface, the behaviour of young people in the 1930s looks much the same as those of today, but there are significant differences. The aim of the former was "a good time" which, if it was to continue to be a good time, meant a good deal of conventional and moral restriction. The modern aim is rather pompously expressed in the existentialist term "authentic existence" which is very different indeed from the "good time". The atheistic existentialism of, for example, Sartre, is just as different from the naïve anti-religiousness of Bernard Shaw, or for that matter, of the superficiality of current humanism. The despairing pathos of Sartre, or the passionate zest of Tennessee Williams, are tremendously strong and inspiring things, deep if frustrated quests for reality for which the word "prayer", in Rahner's sense, does not seem wholly inappropriate. But, and here is the crux of the modern problem, prayer weaned away from conventional narrowness and pietism.

It is not within my competence to pursue the possibility of a new "natural prayer" outside the Christian theological context, but it is important to glimpse the possibility, and to see some such need arising from the modern world itself. In the extreme, morality, philosophy, materialism, idealism, socialism, yes and humanism too, are all rejected by modern leaders of thought as inadequate. On the atheistic and agnostic levels it would seem that a new kind of pagan mysticism is being sought. I can only confine my speculations to Christian prayer, but not only is it important to set this in the wider context, but this context itself rightly impinges upon the trends discernible in Christian spirituality. For here, too, is found a broadening, a movement away from formal spiritual exercises towards the quest for a deeper continuity of total life in God. There is a move away from rigid definition of type and method in prayer towards a greater freedom and a more adventurous spirit of experiment: the liturgical movement forms an obvious example. There is a move away from prayer as "duty to God", in obedience to an external command, towards a more virile sense of response to the living God as primal human need. There is also a move from, in technical terms, the speculative to the affective, and coupled with it from meditative reasoning to contemplative experience. This all impinges on modern thought in that it is a way from discursive reason issuing in substantive statements to existential experience issuing in a deepening of spiritual insights and intuitions. The aim to which Christian spirituality is groping would seem to be best expressed not so much as moral perfection, or knowledge of God, or duty to God—though it will contain all these—but as Rahner's "receptive spirituality" or Ramsey's "cosmic disclosure". It is a deepening of responsiveness to divine action in a continuum of living.

So we must ask again, in the narrower context of Christian theology, what is prayer and what has theology to say about its continuing development? How can theology nurture and guide it? These questions lead to further experiments with pastoral and applied theology, for it is only through prayer that theology impinges upon experience.

On the simplest level kneeling in church and addressing words to God, or meditating on the Bible, or contemplating a crucifix, would be universally regarded as prayer. A country walk during which one continually thought about God would not be regarded as prayer. Yet to most religious people the former kind of activity would constitute a somewhat restricted use of the term, while the latter would seem to be stretching the word too far. Where and how is the line to be drawn? Is saying grace before meals prayer? Is the contemplation of a crucifix prayer and the contemplation of a daffodil not prayer? Spiritual theology resolves this problem, but in so doing it creates two others bearing on the practical adaptation of tradition to the needs and outlook of modern people. These problems must, therefore, in their turn be subjected to theology for their solution.

Spiritual theology resolves the problem by dividing a total Christian life into two separate yet interrelated things: "prayer" and "recollection". The first is then satisfactorily restricted to formal spiritual exercises while the second embraces the whole of life lived, consciously or subconsciously, in and with Jesus Christ. This is, in modern jargon, the life or total commitment or of existential confrontation. But spiritual theology also insists that the two are related in terms of process and product: it is only through the disciplined and systematic use of formal prayer that recollection—commitment—grows into a deep and constant state. Here the two new problems arise although, as I hope to show, they are not so new as to be beyond solution by the application of traditional doctrine.

The first problem is that the modern desire is for the recollected life, for Christian faith expressed in the world rather than in the sanctuary, for practice not piety; and there is a corresponding reaction against formal prayer in the narrower sense. I have attempted to clarify this dilemma elsewhere, pointing out the impossibility of hoping for the end-product while eliminating the process (*The Rock and The River*, chap. 5). But is it possible to accept modern aspiration with sympathy, and can spiritual theology offer any alleviation to the man who sincerely wants to be a loyal disciple of Christ but who is not attracted by formal piety? I think it can.

Christian history and theology leave no doubt that "prayer" as the producer of recollection—Christian living—consists in a threefold complex made up of the holy eucharist, the divine office, and uniquely personal devotion to Christ, all with their specific interrelations and emphases. But Christian theology and tradition is equally emphatic that, while prayer and worship have autonomous value, any system of formal religious exercises is only a means to an end. To St. Benedict, the eucharist and the divine office was verily *opus Dei*, it was in itself the work of God, and yet it led necessarily to total recollection, to a higher end, which was a continuum of practical discipleship. Thus scholarship, craftmanship, and manual labour were neither practicalities nor a discontinuous relief from formal prayer, but a veritable part of the Benedictine Rule itself. Similarly almsgiving, hospitality and pastoral service were not only practical duties but integral parts of the Rule of which *opus Dei* was the foundation.

Christian life and love can be nothing less than the life and love of the risen Christ manifested through his disciples by their response to grace. This response is initially made through formal prayer guided by theology, and the fundamental complex of eucharist, office and personal devotion is nothing if not theological. Although this pattern is fundamental in structure, it has varied enormously in detail throughout Christian history. If, therefore, modern man is more attracted to product than to process, more to Christian living than to piety, more to existential spontaneity than to formal duty, then he wants to ask, and ought to ask what is the *efficient minimum framework* of formal prayer which can by God's grace produce the end-product? Regrettably the question is not asked because it sounds impious and would no doubt shock the vicar, but it is not only a good question but a traditional one. When it is emancipated from senti-mentality (how can one think of giving a minimum to God?), from the "going-to-church" complex, and from pietism, ascetical theology has never hesitated to indulge in a little down-to-earth time and motion study. St. Bernard, in his famous controversy with Peter of Cluny, objected not only to Cluniac wealth and magnificence but to the fact that too much time was spent in chapel and not enough in the harvest fields.

The current problem may best be explained by analogy. The medieval builder had little knowledge of engineering in the sense of the relation between the strength of materials and the strains and stresses they had to bear. So he erred on the safe side, very well on the safe side: he was content to make a good strong job and leave it at that. An architect has told me that, in the average Tudor timber framed house, the upright studs are absurdly close

together, and the roof beams far too thick. The builder no
doubt calculated that timbers three feet apart would
probably do, so he spaced them one foot apart; a beam
six inches square ought to support the roof, so he found
one two feet square. The finished house looked, and was,
extremely solid and beautiful, but it was, strictly speaking,
inefficient because a vast amount of material was superfluous. With all respect, it might be suggested that the
Benedictine sevenfold office was something rather like
that, it made a good strong job of supporting continuous
recollection: you cannot spend all that time singing
psalms and immediately forget all about God in the
intervals. But Cranmer, with a brilliant piece of ascetical
engineering, concluded that a couple of slightly thicker
posts seven feet apart would support just as much as
seven stakes one foot apart: morning and evening prayer
is an efficient substitute for the breviary sequence. I
think Anglican history, especially in its best periods, has
proved Cranmer right.

But if St. Benedict was dealing with sixth-century
monks in a monastery, Cranmer legislated for sixteenth-
century peasants in a village. The current task of ascetical
theology—or engineering—is to provide adequately and
efficiently for twentieth-century men on the move.
Cranmer's pastoral concern nevertheless led him into
ascetical error. The two essential emphases of the divine
office are that it is the corporate prayer of the Church
(whether recited in choir or in private makes no difference) and that it is offered as pure praise to God the
Father Almighty through Jesus Christ. In order that
sixteenth-century peasants should enjoy the fruits of a
richer life of prayer, Cranmer complicated the office by
adding all kinds of elements which have no right to be
there, and thereby overlaid both essential emphases of
corporateness and objectivity, while pastoral practice

today has continued this process to a state of chaos. The original corner post is so overlaid with struts, ornaments and decoration that its real purpose is forgotten. Conservatives swoon in ecstasy at its beauty—"the incomparable heritage of the Book of Common Prayer"—while radicals denounce its archaism—"modern people cannot understand it". Both overlook the prior question: What is it *for*? Let us be honest: if the constant repetition of a curious translation of a set of ancient religious folk-songs, interspersed with doubtful legends relating to a primitive tribe, is the Church's way of inspiring love, devotion, intellectual understanding and religious edification, then the Church is not just out of date, it is insane. In fact the Church is remarkably sane and to the point. The Anglican office, the need for revision notwithstanding, is still a supreme vehicle for corporate and objective praise, which is all it is *for*. Both conservative eulogy and radical criticism springs from the failure to get beyond straight theology to its subtler and more creative uses.

The modern Christian is neither monk nor peasant but a responsible and intelligent disciple who wants to live the Christian life of penitence, joy, intercession, praise, service, faith and love. And he wants to see this more as an existential continuum and less as a series of formal devotions. He knows perfectly well that this is impossible without the grace of the sacraments, but he is not always aware that his aspiration, legitimate as it is, lies under the perennial danger of immanentalism, of a *shallow* worldliness. He is also disastrously mobile and, as a Christian, very much alone in an antagonistic secularism. The divine office, with its double corporate-transcendent emphasis, is exactly what he needs. He does *not* need Cranmer's sixteenth-century elaborations. I conclude that for modern people a much shorter and simpler twofold daily office (or a threefold office after the

Cistercian *conversi* pattern might be a worthy experiment) is a legitimate need. It is a legitimate need *not* because modern man is busy or anxious or burdened with practical difficulties, but because he is a modern man. Such shortening and simplification is in no way a matter of modification or relaxation of the rules; it is the conclusion of spiritual theology applied and used, the conclusion of ascetical time and motion study. But if something of this sort is to be a creative experiment two things are necessary: the old theological emphases of corporateness and transcendence must be stressed and all others rigorously rejected, and the Franciscan-Jesuit principle of "private" recitation accepted in full. To pretend that in modern Anglican practice mattins and evensong are "choir offices", or worse "church services", is to be ascetically in error and pastorally blind. The liturgical powers that be might at least realise that for every time the divine office is sung in church it is recited privately on many thousands of occasions.

If, then, the serious modern Christian can be assisted by the calm quest for a theological minimum of formal prayer, the second problem arises. Granted that habitual recollection, continuous Christian living, can only be built on the foundation of formal prayer, is it possible to assist such existential awareness of the presence of Christ by the application of theology? Given an efficient minimum framework of formal prayer must recollection be left to grow of itself or can it be directly encouraged? We all know of regrettable examples when the converse is true; when in spite of much disciplined prayer, worship and formal meditation, the spirit of Christ somehow fails to show itself in a man's life and work. Ascetical regula, like sacramental grace, is an essential foundation, but it is not magic. There must be a volitional response, an acceptance. Can *this* be directly encouraged? Given the foundation, is it possible to nurture a theological outlook which can assist Christian living?

The question may be put thus: if formal prayer is the mainspring of Christian life in the world, is there any way in which Christian living can inspire formal prayer? I think the answer may be affirmative when the two are seen to be complementary and interactive. Anglican tradition inclines to the view that prayer guides life rather than that, as in certain other schools of spirituality, the main purpose of life is a preparation for prayer. But we are really speaking of a circular movement, or even of a paradox. I think the Anglican emphasis is basically right, Christian life is, or should be, a full-blooded thing manifesting positive virtues and accomplishments like love, service, creativity and craftsmanship. It cannot validly be reduced to a preparation for spiritual exercises. On the other hand, the eucharist can hardly be regarded as only a help or springboard for life's practical duties. Now I think this problem might be resolved by seriously taking into account the double implication of Incarnational doctrine. In the words of the *Quicunque Vult:* "Man, of the substance of his Mother, born in the world" and yet: "One, not by conversion of the Godhead into flesh: but by taking of the Manhood into God." If spatial metaphor is still permissible, Christ came down in order that men should go up. This could mean that although formal prayer remains the foundation of Christian life to come, it is also backward-looking. In practice a Christian begins his day at the altar mainly thinking about God's activity in his life yesterday. The eucharist is not primarily that which inspires future action but that which sanctifies the past, lifting it up into the redemptive stream. Similarly a retreat, rather than being a period of spiritual refreshment and inspiration for the future, is predominantly a contemplative consummation of what has gone before.

So while a minimal system of formal prayer remains a Christian's first duty and the foundation of his practical life, his life, rather than being a preparation for prayer, is fully sanctified and consummated by it. The importance of everyday experience can then be seen as rebounding to the inspiration of prayer without losing its value or overthrowing the proper regula-recollection order and relation. We may, therefore, freely look to theology to assist our lives, to help our recollection, to bless our true worldliness, to sanctify the secular, without risking the errors of immanentalism, Pelagianism, activism and all the rest, which surely creep in whenever formality in prayer and worship fall out of relation with Christian life.

There is, moreover, a further paradox. To a mature Christian, regula—a formal complex of prayer—leads into recollection—the sanctification of worldly experience. But this is obviously reversed in the case of conversion, or even of the progress from spiritual childhood to maturity. Initial spiritual insights, the first intuitive confrontation with Christ, primary religious stirrings, are all plainly mediated through creation, not by learning creeds. It is only when the gift of faith has been received that creeds can function in the development and formulation of that faith through prayer. Spirituality, as St. Thomas insists, begins with sense-experience.

We may, therefore, look to theology to help the development of a spirituality consistent with modern thought and ambition. And we need not fear if it begins with worldly life and experience, for this is not only legitimate but it offers the best chance of formulating new types of formal prayer as well as directly assisting secular life.

CHAPTER SEVEN

Pastoral Theological Method

The most significant difference between the disciplines
of scholarship and pastoral theology is that the former
looks forward on a narrow front while the latter looks
backward as broadly as possible. Although some historical
background is necessary to scholarship it consists largely
in picking up the contemporary trend somewhere in the
immediate past and progressing onward to new hypotheses and new conclusions. Modern biblical studies might
begin with Karl Barth but they need not necessarily go
back to biblical thought in the eighteenth century. The
material selected, however, has to be studied in minute
detail, and with current specialisation little heed need be
taken of other branches of theology. A scholar's field
narrows still further as he advances: from the study of the
bible in general, the would-be scholar has to choose
between Old and New Testaments and finally he selects a
single book, part of a book, or theme upon which to
concentrate his attention.

Pastoral theology, on the other hand, starts with the
broadest possible sweep of the whole of theology framed
within ecclesiastical history. Compared with scholarship
it must be and should be superficial, although the acquisition of such a range on any level would constitute no
mean task over a course of three or four years. Such an
approach should not be considered in any way inferior to

scholarship; their function is different and yet, by *use*, they become complementary. The scholar is concerned with new hypotheses and new truth, whatever it be and however it may arise: whether this new truth is immediately useful in pastoral practice is not his concern although, if he is a faithful member of the body of Christ, he should hope that it may become usable at some time or in some place. The pastoral theologian, however, having fulfilled his initial studies, begins his creative work by taking stock of the existential situation, noting its hopes and fears and the problems they create, and then looking over the widest sweep of his pastoral theological knowledge for clues towards their solution. In the properly trained pastoral theologian, this process should lead to a series of intuitions, insights or "hunches" which will guide and direct his more detailed studies. It should be unnecessary to add that such insights, intuitions or hunches are unlikely to arise except under the influence of prayer as I have attempted to describe it. Neither will any conclusions he may reach be of practical value to modern Christians unless they are harnessed to the needs of prayer in this broad sense and convertible through prayer into action.

Let us then attempt an experiment in pastoral theology towards possible solutions of some of the problems of prayer now current.

Beginning with the existential situation, certain facts, reactions, likes and dislikes of modern people have been unearthed. The tendency is towards expressing Christianity in the work-a-day world rather than by formal devotional exercises. A corresponding trend is towards forms of prayer which concern in existential terms the whole man, not some hypothetical "spiritual" aspect of him. There is therefore a reaction not so much against "dogma" as against intellectualism. In terms of ascetical theology this means recollection rather than formal prayer, contemplative awareness rather than discursive meditation. Corollary to these characteristics of the modern Christian outlook are stresses on individuality within the Church rather than the corporate nature of the Church itself, and on the immanence rather than the transcendence of God. It is with this practical situation that pastoral theology must begin, and a prior question is an enquiry into its health and legitimacy. Are these aspirations and interests acceptable to theology, and capable of being used, harnessed and sanctified? Or are they modern perversions of true religion to be eradicated or at least corrected? Are we right in looking to theology to help modern man as he is, or is this but a weak pandering to his whims? We begin, in other words, with the broad backcloth of *negative* or *testing* theology.

A wide purview of Christian history suggests that this modern outlook is justified, but with certain safeguards. The Church has never been happy with mere pietism and has always extolled practical Christian service. There have been schools of thought and spirituality within Christian tradition stressing individuality, the divine immanence, anti-intellectualism, and all of these schools have produced their saints. On the other hand, some of these characteristics have led to error, especially individualism, immanentalism, and the minimising of the significance of the Church's corporate discipline. These factors need correction and I have argued (in this book and elsewhere) that such correction is supplied by an insistence on the traditional and theological threefold foundation of Christian life. Personal life with Christ in the world is balanced by binding the prayer proper to it with the eucharist and the divine office. We are not, however, pandering to modern weakness in considering his formal and corporate prayer in terms of an efficient

theological minimum. A man who prefers bread and
meat to green vegetables risks vitamin deficiency which
has to be taken seriously but little purpose is served by
forcing hundredweights of cabbage down his throat.

Having thus examined modern trends, themselves
questions of insight, discussion and pastoral observation,
our task is to look back over the broadest sweep of historical theology in an attempt to unearth some teaching,
some inspiration, which seems relevant. First, what is
the essential Christian doctrine that may throw light on
the problem? My hunch would be that, thinking in terms
of total existential awareness of God immanent in the
world, recollection not formality of devotion, the concrete
situation not doctrinal abstraction, one might do worse
than start with the doctrine of creation itself.

God made the world and he made it very good. That is
the main contention of patristic theology against all
dualistic systems and consistently held in spite of the
difficulties arising with the problem of sin and evil. So
the universe manifests the goodness of God sacramentally,
but how are we to approach it in and through prayer,
with intuition, insight and inspiration? We are led to
look to those saints and teachers in the Church's history
who were concerned with both Christian prayer and the
doctrine of creation: Hugh of St. Victor, Francis of Assisi,
Thomas Aquinas.

Hugh of St. Victor elaborated a scheme of prayer
based on the contemplation of the natural world. I have
no doubt that it has much to teach modern Christians
about their approach to the universe, about the relation
of religion with science, and indeed about Christian
prayer. Here at last is a system of spirituality that begins
and ends, not in the sanctuary, but in the world, which
accepts the primacy of sense-experience over "detachment
from creatures", and which might well act as counter to

much abstractive devotional idiom that modern people (including myself) find infuriating. If we move from pastoral to applied theology, there would be few modern Christians who could not safely be advised to read and meditate on this scheme of prayer. But, keeping to the discipline of pastoral theology, it must be concluded that Hugh of St. Victor by no means answers the whole problem. His scheme, though in the world, is still a formal progression from one stage to another, and although his insights may well inspire, I can imagine very few modern Christians happily accepting and using his system as a whole. Moreover, while his approach to creation is generally contemplative it assumes a good deal of discursive meditation and its end-product though avowedly "contemplation" is likely to be doctrine rather than an opening-up of intuitive insights of love; an openness to the existential reality of God.

As with Hugh of St. Victor, much inspiration may well arise out of the creation doctrine of St. Thomas: the idea of a hierarchy of being; of the true reality of creatures against the somewhat shadowy "mirrored reflection" of Hugh; the glory given to God by each species after its kind; the "potentiality" of nature and its perfection by grace. All this is worth study by modern man in search of an ascetic of creation and then of a this-worldly prayer.

But the same difficulties arise in a more serious form: St. Thomas says much about creation and much about prayer, but there is little obvious connection. The doctrine of analogy is of tremendous significance to modern life but the Thomist hierarchy is too definite, too rigid, and finally too metaphysical. Can pastoral theology get over this difficulty?

St. Francis of Assisi looks like a worthwhile hunch. It is sometimes forgotten that St. Francis' poverty was an ascetical not a moral concept, and it was also a thoroughly world-affirming idea. St. Francis' religion, writes Father Cuthbert, "did not raise a barrier between him and the earth, but the earth itself became transformed in his sight and gave him a new joy." (*Life of St. Francis of Assisi*, pp. 26–7.) Is not this something like modern man's ideal? I think so, but again we are offered little more than theories. It is significant, however, that St. Francis, like modern existentialist thinkers, and also like certain theologians of the linguistic school, chooses to offer his spiritual insights not in substantive doctrine but in poetry. His anti-intellectualism is a refreshing change which points towards the needs of modern people. So is his glorious conception of the contemplative unity of creation, of a harmony with the universe recapitulated in individual things: birds, streams, sun, moon, mountains and people. The contemplation of creatures would appear to offer a start towards a modern recollective technique. But how is this achieved? St. Francis does not tell us. Can anyone else, over the broad sweep of Christian history, come to our aid?

Martin Buber makes his now famous distinction between "I-it" and "I-thou" experience. The first is something akin to scientific study, whether the object is a material thing or another person. The second is a contemplative relation of love, a meeting, a harmony with a creature, a union: "The primary word *I-Thou* can only be spoken with the whole being." Moreover: "The extended lines of relations meet in the eternal Thou. Every particular *Thou* is a glimpse through to the eternal *Thou*." (*I and Thou*, pp. 3, 13, 75). Consciously or otherwise, Buber has moved from Hugh of St. Victor to St. Francis. Hugh's contemplation of the symbolic universe, in spite of a certain reverence, remains very much an I-It relation; it is "scientific" even if its outcome is theology and not natural science. St. Francis' relation with creation

G

and creatures—birds, flowers, lice and all—is gloriously
I-Thou.

Here is a glimmer of light in our search for a modern
ascetical world-outlook, for an existential encounter with
creation as manifesting, and offering a response to, the
love of God. But we have not got further than theism:
how does Christ come into this picture? In thinking of
St. Francis I had to use the word "recapitulation" to
describe his contemplative love for creation summed up
in an individual thing. A pastoral theological hunch
suggests a look at this word as it is especially conceived
in the theology of St. Irenaeus.

To Irenaeus Christ is not only the "champion" of mankind, recapitulating, or re-living the life of Adam in
victory instead of defeat, but he is verily the second Adam
of St. Paul. Christ "recapitulates" humanity within
himself, he is truly the new humanity, the creator of a new
race. But it is a mistake to divorce humanity from creation,
and so recapitulation and redemption extend to the whole
of creation: things as well as people. This too is Pauline:
the whole creation which "groaneth and travaileth in
pain together until now" must itself share in the mystery
of the resurrection of the body: only then shall God be all
in all. This is the particular message of the Christianisation
of Buber by Karl Heim (see *The World: its Creation and
Consummation*), and it is a concept which, though continuously held in the contemplative East, is now returning
to theological interest in Western Christian thought
(e.g. W. Kunneth, *The Theology of the Resurrection*). But
we still need Irenaeus to translate a theistic conception of
nature into Christian recollective contemplation. If all
creation is recapitulated in the incarnate Lord then it
now shares in the redemptive process. If the Incarnation
and Resurrection change the very status of mankind they
also affect the material world of things. So creatures no

longer manifest only the mind of the creator, they also mediate the redeeming Christ. The Resurrection has its effects on apple trees, and—always supported by the foundation of office, eucharist and personal devotion— apple trees contemplated in an I-Thou relation becomes not natural but truly Christian prayer. And the same should apply to telephones, tables and typewriters.

The final question now poses itself: can such in-the-world recollection help modern man to realise his existential confrontation with the person of the risen Christ himself? Have we here the seeds of a substitute for Ignatian-type meditation which is both out of step with modern biblical studies and unpopular with contemporary men? For it is an undisputable pastoral fact that the old "three-point" meditation, based on the naïve assumption that a living image of the man Jesus emerges from the gospel narrative, is something that very few modern people can make. And this is not suprising if note is taken of the scholar's difficulties with the "historical Jesus". What is crystal clear is that the New Testament contains not a syllable of physical description of our Lord's person, in which case the Ignation "image" cannot be of the first importance. It would appear that the pastoral error (which I have frequently made myself) was to compare the New Testament with a novel in the teaching of meditation. The suggestion is that by the use of the imagination the hero of a novel is clearly discerned, and that the central figure of the gospel should be equally plain. Tension, "Bible-study", and a sort of "Bible-phobia", have all been indicted as responsible for the frustration of this simple idea. But it has been curiously overlooked that a novel contains skilled description of the hero's appearance while the gospels contain none at all. On the other hand our knowledge of Plato, Shakespeare or Confucius as *people* arises almost entirely from a study of their works and not from straight description or doubtful pictorial representation. The New Testament is unique, yet to compare it with a play, or an historical record, or a work of philosophy, or better perhaps as a synthesis of them all, may be a better meditative approach than the fictional hero analogy. This is in line with the biblical movement usually referred to as the "new quest for the historical Jesus". As we learn of Caesar's character from his exploits, of Shakespeare's from his plays, of Hume's from his works, so the character, the real personality if not the physical image of Jesus is discernible from his history, activities and sayings as recorded in the gospels.

In *The Rock and The River*, (pp. 81–97) I suggested that both from the viewpoint of modern scholarship and of the modern outlook, meditative prayer should begin with the existential experience of the "Christ of faith" and return to the New Testament in order to clothe this divine confrontation with humanity—the reverse process of the Ignatian method. Thus the natural starting point for meditation is not the Bible but the eucharist. But, more especially in view of modern aspiration, we can go further than this. The modern worldly-recollective *attrait* naturally seeks the sacred humanity of Christ manifested in his Church, that is in his disciples: in people. The danger here is that in isolation, "seeking Christ in others" soon degenerates into immanentalism or even sentimentality. Matthew 25. 31–46, Luke 9. 47–8, and Matthew 12. 46–50 are much more than simple ethical directives. They are concerned with the doctrine of the Church as grounded in the sacred humanity; and we move back to the re-capitulation doctrine of St. Irenaeus.

Another devastating criticism of Ignatian meditation is that it assumes a living fellowship with the historical Jesus as portrayed (or asssumed to be portrayed) in the days of his earthly ministry. Our existential fellowship, however, is with the risen and glorified Lord manifested in Church, Scripture, humanity and creation. Rightly assuming continuity of person from the Incarnation to the Ascension, even a detailed description of Jesus handed down from an eyewitness (which we do not have) would be an insufficient basis for recollective experience today. But if all creation is recapitulated in the sacred humanity, if apple trees and typewriters are part of the ultimate redemption in Christ, how much more are persons a true manifestation of the sacred humanity in daily life? If we gain the recollective state wherein ugliness in creation and sin in people both in their different ways show forth the Cross, and beauty and sanctity give us glimpses of the ascended redeemer, then we have moved far away from the prevalent superficiality of "seeing Christ in others".

It is frequently argued that some Ignatian-type "image" of Jesus is still necessary to safeguard the doctrine of the true humanity; that its absence inevitably opens the flood-gates of Apollinarianism, thence puritanism and a false other-worldliness. This carries weight, but in view of our discussion so far, and in face of the fact that the gospels give us no help whatever to formulate such an image, I am led to revise my former opinion and wonder whether this argument has been allowed to carry too much weight? The sacred humanity *must* be safeguarded in Christian prayer and experience: a woolly abstraction of "humanity", a disembodied series of "characteristics", a vague aura of piety, do not add up to a *person*, and nothing less than confrontation with the living *person* of Jesus in prayer and life will ultimately do. But is not the recollective sense of the manifestation of Christ in people, *plus* the experiential encounter in the eucharist, *plus* reference to the gospel for intuitive insight into the character of our Lord—is not this living synthesis of prayer—this regula—sufficient in itself? I think it probably is, but if not, the meditative *use* of Christological doctrine, even the *use* of Chalcedonian Christology by "absorption", should provide sufficient safeguard.

Our experiment in pastoral theologising has, then, issued in something like a new construction in spiritual theology, but one which retains all the orthodox elements —eucharist, divine office, devotion and recollection— but in a different combination. This new order, this new set of relationships, these new emphases, spring from serious consideration of modern people *as they are*.

In the next chapter I shall try to reduce this speculation to direct, down-to-earth pastoral terms. But whatever the value, or lack of value, in my own experiment and its results, even if it turns out to be completely useless it might still serve as a pattern or demonstration of how to *do* pastoral theology. If this helps to lead others to use theology in this way, and to wean some away from the idolatry of "scholarship", then the value of my own conclusions is of little account.

CHAPTER EIGHT

Theology and a Happy Asceticism

Ascetical theology means, primarily, the doctrine, method and technique of prayer, and only secondly does it include those disciplines which support and nurture it. The foundation of Christian life, flowing through prayer, is the threefold complex of the eucharist, the divine office and personal devotion. This leads into a true Christian affirmation of creation—a proper "worldliness"—which is technically called habitual recollection. This fundamental regula is necessary because it expresses the doctrine of the Holy Trinity and it maintains the doctrine of grace to which prayer is response. But the modern Christian is more interested in expressing his faith in life than in formal prayer, which is a legitimate outlook. And he thinks of a necessary minimum of formal prayer as inspired by his experience in the world, which is strictly orthodox. Re-collection is the product of regula, but if prayer begins with sense experience, there is a sense in which a recol-lected life rebounds to inspire formal prayer. Ultimately we have a circular movement, and it does not matter very much where one begins to draw a circle. So in an attempt to construct a modern spirituality it seems wise to start with the modern man's main interest: "in the world". We start, in other words, with the secondary aspect of ascetical theology, with the recollective tech-niques and disciplines which support prayer.

Concupiscence, in its proper meaning of psychological disharmony, makes discipline and mortification necessary in support of Christian prayer. Traditional disciplines like fasting may still have their place in this or any other age. But such disciplines must be linked with prayer or they become at best legalistic or at worst ridiculous. Whatever degree of world-affirmation is accepted, there will still be a place for mortification which is devotionally penitential. A good deal more will be necessarily remedial, and other types aid recollection, like the traditional Friday fast. But Christian *askesis*—the training of the spiritual athlete—means more than that. It has its positive side in supporting and nurturing prayer by harnessing natural *attrait*, and it must never be allowed to degenerate into the popular idea of useless austerity. Indeed, there is a good deal of the harnessing of *attrait* in the Church's more austere saints: they obviously enjoyed austerity! In this deeper and more accurate sense, is it possible to construct a modern ascetic; one that will creatively nurture modern prayer and which will be acceptable to modern men? For a true ascetic must be acceptable, not in the sense of easy or comfortable but in the sense of that which appears to be worthwhile, which subserves a positive purpose. Is there a system of recollective discipline which might first harness the right modern aims and secondly eliminate those aspects of modern life which are clearly contrary to the development of Christian life?

In *Christian Spirituality Today*, Professor Demant has gone some way to deal with the second point. Primarily he advocates a discipline of mind which accepts the facts and limitations of human existence and which divides into four positive disciplines. First: "some conscious discrimination between the multifarious stimuli offered to our minds and hearts, and a refusal to be subject to a good many of them." Second: "disciplines allied to the quest for solitude, contemplation and thought." Third: "a religious discipline as consumers", implying a sane discrimination between advertisements and a refusal to be dictated to by the commercial whims of vogue and fashion. Demant here accepts both true asceticism coupled with a right worldliness, or even a right "materialism", which well demonstrates the real meaning of *askesis*: "To give preference to good food, good houses, good clothes, good furniture, over status-enhancing, wealth-flaunting, smartness-flashing acquisitions, would be a right kind of materialism." His fourth point is concerned with vocational choice.

This is valuable so far as it goes, but with the exception of the second point, it remains weighted on the negative side. A more serious criticism is that Demant veers towards the fundamental trap of not really *using* theology and thus risking the disastrous divorce between ascetic and ethic. There is no doubt that we should all be better for following his advice, but this is qualified by a moral, rather than an ascetical-moral "ought" (again with the exception of the second point). He is saying that we ought to do these things in the sense that children ought to obey their parents, not, which is what we need, in the sense that as an athlete has trained properly he *ought* to win. Can this be improved upon?

Professor Demant's second, and most constructive point is nevertheless weakened by seeing the outcome of solitude entirely in terms of social morality. It is no more than "welcome" when families, for example, begin to live as families, doing things and conversing together instead of pursuing the frantic search for mass entertainment. Yet the idea behind this—if I may say so without offence—rather flat statement at least gives us a pastoral "hunch": in fact it takes us back to St. Irenaeus, Heim and Buber.

According to the traditional interpretation of the creation stories in Genesis, God made the universe and then "rested". The Sabbath tradition flows through Christian history mainly as an ascetical not as a moral concept, and it implies the continuation of an active contemplative love which keeps all things in being. Thus contemplation is the proper consummation of all activity: hence the looking *back* in retreat and in eucharistic worship. It is in this sense of the divine love maintaining a continuous creative activity in the universe that Christians think of "seeing God in creation". The Christian doctrine therefore differs from the quasi-deistic analogies wherein God is related to his creation as an artist is to his picture, or, as in Hugh of St. Victor, as an author's mind is manifested in his book. There is some truth in this idea but it is ultimately deistic: a painter can sell his picture and have no more to do with it, an author can forget all about his book once it is published. But unless we are occasionalists the universe continues to exist only by the contemplative love of God.

The Irenaean tradition goes further. The Sabbath which consummates creation is fulfilled by the liturgical "Greater Sabbath"—Holy Saturday—which consummates redemption: from the tomb Christ contemplates in love his redemptive victory. Thus, by the doctrine of recapitulation, or of Christ the second Adam, the whole creation participates in the unfolding redemptive economy of the Holy Trinity. All things must finally be consummated in glory. And men, at one with nature and in Christ, can co-operate in this ultimate redemptive process. It is often suggested that a farmer, for example, "co-operates with God" in creating fertility and its products. But this suffers from the same faults as the artist-picture analogy: it is basically deistic and frequently sentimental. But there remains a grain of truth which may grow like the parabolic mustard seed if it is harnessed to serious prayer. How can this be done?

Orthodoxy teaches that the most elementary type of religious experience, the "first form of contemplation" consists in that sense of unity with an environment supremely illustrated in the all-embracing love of St. Francis of Assisi. I suggest that the first ascetical discipline necessary for the achievement of this contemplative awareness is that of *making* an environment. The second necessity is loving contemplation of what one has made. A great deal of sentimentality is evoked by the idea of God in nature—"you are nearer to God in a garden than anywhere else on earth"—and of the spiritual value of craftsmanship. But again there are truths in these ideas; the sentimentality arises from the omission of any serious idea of prayer and its necessary discipline. To be in a garden, especially a strange garden, and to look at it with whatever admiration and aesthetic satisfaction, is essentially an I-It relation. And a few pious thoughts about God do not add very much to the experience. But if you have made the garden, entering a loving relation with each part of it, you begin to feel the sense of oneness with it as a whole. Instead of units of beds, shrubs, lawns and hedges, the garden becomes an environment, and if this is contemplated you feel "at home" in it, at peace with it, joyful in it. And that is very near to elementary contemplation. It is significant that Dr. Mascall, in his recent Boyle lectures (published under the title *The Christian Universe*), frequently describes today's frustrated secularism as a sense of "homelessness", which is the opposite of contemplation. Now if our hypothetical gardener is a Christian who has "absorbed" in formal prayer, first the implications of the Christian Sabbath tradition, then the recapitulation doctrine wherein his garden partakes of the redemption of our Lord, and if he sees the immanence of the Holy Spirit in connection with this, then he is not very far from the first revelation of Julian of Norwich: "Suddenly the Trinity filled my heart with utmost joy".

Such a conception still depends upon a man's constant response to his faith in the Holy Trinity through the Church's threefold regula. There is no short cut. But have we here the beginnings of an ascetical discipline which might support, interact with, and make sense of, these necessary formal duties which otherwise seem a meaningless burden to modern people?

Professor Demant has spoken of the moral satisfaction arising from families staying at home and doing things together. Can we not go further? During the difficult period just after the last war a domestic movement grew up called "do-it-yourself". Men and women of all classes and types spent their weekends painting, papering and mending furniture. The original circumstances have now changed but this movement continues unabated: people are still "doing-it-themselves" without reference to commercial or economic need. They like it. Is this curious social development a question of habit, recreation, or could it be providential? Are men groping after the satisfaction of being "at home" in an environment they have created? Have I perhaps misinterpreted Demant's word "satisfaction" in family life? Alternatively, should not he have gone further and spoken of contemplative love? Could there be a sense here where sociology, even so-called Christian sociology, fails in its approach to modern man by not going anything like far enough to satisfy his needs? We are so wrapped up in the morality of "decent working conditions" that we see the office canteen, the factory playing-field, the works dance, as no more than social amenities. Such things could be significant to ascetical theology! If this appears far-fetched the use of theology that arrived at the possibility seems to me to be more orthodox and potentially more fruitful than rigging up a factory chapel and employing a factory chaplain. The sociological implications of all this are frightening in their enormity.

If asceticism in the more usual sense of self-discipline is required in this connection, some curb is needed on the modern passion for aimless movement. Whatever the truth about God and the garden the man initiating an I-Thou relation with an environment by mowing his lawn is certainly spiritually better off than his neighbour's very much I-It relation with the car in front on a jammed highway. All that too is part of God's creation, and it certainly needs redeeming, but I myself find it exceptionally difficult to approach a row of crawling lorries with loving contemplation. It might be recalled that, counter to some of the later spiritualities of other-worldly detachment, Benedictine stability assured a full-blooded love for the whole monastery: buildings, fields, gardens and all. Was not this contemplative harmony created by stability and manual labour? The Benedictines were the most thorough-going exponents of "do-it-yourself", and their motives were not entirely pragmatic.

Professor Demant's most constructive point in his speculations toward a modern asceticism was discipline needed in the creation and use of solitude and silence. This is absolutely necessary as an element in the consummation of activity by contemplation: the unity in love with an environment that one has made. It could constitute another mortification for modern people if it is assumed that silence and solitude are foreign to their nature. But is this a valid assumption? If we are thinking of aspiring Christian people the fantastic progress of the retreat movement casts considerable doubt upon it. Is this, like "do-it-yourself", another subconscious groping after a spiritual reality? For the two have something in common: it is in retreat more than anywhere else that the Franciscan ideal is realised. To repeat the quotation from Father Cuthbert: "St. Francis' religion did not raise a barrier between him and the earth, but the earth itself became transformed in his sight and gave him a new joy". Without any specially unusual sort of "mysticism" this is precisely what often happens in retreat. Creation takes on a new reality, things look different and mean more; we are at one with our environment.

This experience, however, depends upon retreat being properly interpreted. Like all Christian spirituality it must be grounded in the liturgy and the divine office; its emphasis is largely backward-looking, not a period of spiritual refreshment aimed at work to come so much as a contemplative consummation of what has passed, a true sabbath. Nevertheless, when such a technique is accepted, its value for future progress is considerable. For by it we can learn much about the contemplative approach to creation in general; we may learn how to consummate our lawn-mowing and paper-hanging: we are introduced to an I-Thou relation with creatures.

At this point, if not before, I should expect the modern Christian reader to become a little impatient: is not Christianity concerned about people? With loving your neighbour? So why all this ascetical speculation and technique concerned with things? To this I maintain that we have started in the right place. In the Boyle Lectures Dr. Mascall writes: "Man, then, is a social being, and lives in a social context. Nevertheless it is a sheer mistake to suppose that his relationships are purely social ones and that he can fulfil himself by attending exclusively to the latter. By the very fact that he has a body, he is part of the world of nature as well as of the world of persons . . . It is, I think, surprising how little attention some of our secularists, with the great stress they place on existential personal relationships, seem to give to this equally obvious fact, especially since they are only too ready to appeal to the discoveries and assumptions of science against the doctrines of religion. For if there is anything on which scientists seem to be more or less agreed, it is that the human species is organically related to the evolutionary process of the planet on which it lives and, behind that, to the physical universe as a whole. No philosophy of human life can be adequate if it concentrates simply on the relationship in which the individual stands to other human individuals and ignores that in which he stands to the entire universe.

"It is, I think, the recognition of this fact, after decades of neglect in religious circles, that mainly accounts for the extraordinary vogue at the present day of the Jesuit anthropologist and mystic, Pierre Teilhard de Chardin."

It is the neglect of this obvious fact that has also caused much modern prayer, and much of its ascetical support, to become lifeless, legalistic and irrelevant. There can be no doubt that, because of our sin and frailty, a sane modicum of old-fashioned ascetical discipline—of "mortification"—is indispensable to creative prayer. But I believe a tremendous amount of harm has been done by those comparatively modern spiritualities which put all the stress on "detachment from creatures". For Dr. Mascall is supported by the mainstream of the "older spirituality"—which I believe is possessed of the germ of a genuinely new spirituality. St. Benedict, St. Francis, the School of St. Victor and their orthodox mainstream leave no doubt that there is not the remotest possibility of a right relation between persons if those persons do not begin by achieving a right relation with creation.

Dr. Mascall is also right in calling this an *obvious* fact, for it is manifest in all other departments of life. People are interested in where, as well as with whom, they live and work. A man does not usually propose marriage on Paddington station in the rush hour; he seeks out the "ascetical" requirements of silence in an harmonious environment. After which, at a time when one might suppose material things to be singularly unimportant, the couple choose the setting of their honeymoon with considerable care.

Unfortunately, however, we cannot always choose our environment, so we have to *make* it as best we can. Neither can we choose our neighbours, nor our fellow-workers. This, too, calls for ascetical discipline leading to environmental "harmony" before we can truly unite with them by recollective prayer. The snag in the modern ideal of seeing Christ in people, in life not in the sanctuary, is that it assumes all our neighbours and workmates to be Christ-like. Like so many ideals in the so-called new spirituality, the ideal, the end-product, is marvellous but it says practically nothing about the process by which it is to be achieved. Here is another place where the Irenaean coupling of God's creation and Christ's redemption is of value. It is not difficult to see God's hand in a Cotswold pastoral, or an East Anglian sky, or in the Grand Canyon; such sights inspire awe and some sense of contemplation. It is much more difficult to see God in more everyday sights, a concrete office-block, a factory canteen, a typist's desk, let alone in a mangy cat tearing a half-dead mouse to pieces. It is easy enough to see Christ in saints, or in those we love naturally, but much more difficult to discern his spirit in our opponents, rivals or people who get on our nerves. But the redemptive Cross is in all these things and all these people, because the Cross more than anything manifests the real meaning of the love of God. And when all is said and done the contemplation of a cross is the contemplation of a *thing*.

We still have to begin with creation, but fallen creation

which is nevertheless taken up—recapitulated—into the redemptive stream and which will in the end be transformed into glory. Contemplative harmony with an environment is the first ascetical step towards a loving harmony with the people who are organic to it. This exercise will tend towards a recollective discipline which will help towards seeing Christ's redemptive activity at work in all people. If we are unable to see the potential glory of a thistle it is unlikely that we shall see it in a vicious man. St. Francis' love for all people is indissociable from his contemplative love for all creatures—including the lice on his person.

There is nothing startlingly new in all this. In fact, like so much of traditional ascetic, it is old enough to have been smothered by novelties and forgotten. More obviously, there is nothing new in relating asceticism—in the narrower sense—with our relation with creatures. But St. Benedict and St. Francis have been superseded by newer schools of thought teaching a negative doctrine of "detachment". Mortification is still a necessity; certain creatures must be rejected to combat covetousness, no doubt the television must sometimes be switched off to attain silence, and the bar-parlour avoided to attain solitude. But, with St. Francis and St. Benedict, I am suggesting a positive outlook of ascetical significance rather than a negative one which rarely gets beyond moralism.

All this is but the support for that minimum of formal prayer—the modern time and motion study regula—without which Christian life is impossible. It is to be hoped, however, that in starting this way round, with modern man in his existential situation, we might be led to use theology for the working out of a method and approach to formal prayer which will suit him better than the prevailing orthodoxy which he finds difficult and unattractive. It is a mark or true orthodoxy, be it remembered, to *move*.

H

CHAPTER NINE

Theology "Absorbed"

Considered in itself "private prayer" is an abstraction, for it is but one part of an indivisible trinitarian pattern. This does not mean that it cannot be discussed in itself but that any such discussion must continually assume its relation with the eucharist and the divine office, otherwise all kinds of difficulties and dangers creep in. Private prayer, for example, may be quite properly subjective and immanental, but the errors of subjectivism and immanentism must be safeguarded by the opposite emphases of the divine office. Private prayer is also quite properly private, since it is the confrontation between Jesus Christ and unique persons, but this has to be set against the corporate worship of the body of Christ to which uniquely individual Christians all belong. Moreover, private prayer is set in the everyday world and it starts with experience in the world; it is often concerned with worldly things and it assumes, rightly, that God is continuously active in the world, both in creation and redemption. But this makes no religious sense unless God is also conceived as transcendent, outside the world, outside nature altogether; majestic, omnipotent, all glorious.

This is particularly important since the natural emphasis of modern people is this-worldly. I have tried to explain that this modern outlook, in the face of theology

and history, is *legitimate:* no school of spirituality has ever
got things exactly right. But this is why a new stress on
the absolute necessity of liturgical worship is so important.
Granted all that, we are permitted to treat of personal
prayer according to both theology and the modern outlook. But first it is necessary not only to stress the need for
liturgy but also to stress its correct emphases in the light
of this modern situation. I will only repeat here what we
have discovered already. In brief, that eucharistic worship
is a two-way approach to God consonant with the two-way
action of God in incarnation and redemption. Holy
communion indeed offers grace and love to be manifested
in the world, but it is also the means of the Church's
lifting the everyday world into the stream of redemptive
grace: "One; not by conversion of the Godhead into
flesh: but by taking of the Manhood into God." So
whatever the liturgical experts decide—and their studies
are most important—I suggest that, for modern Christians,
the second is the more meaningful approach. It is one
which begins in the world with immanence and leads
onward to a lifting-up to God transcendent, which is a
good way round; healthier in fact than attempting to fix
the mind on transcendence with one eye on the world all
the time. A little while ago pious direction suggested that
one should make acts of recollection by looking back to
one's last communion; today it would seem more realistic
to begin with experience in everyday life and look forward
to the next communion when this past experience would
be consummated in love. Conversely, immediate preparation used to be concerned almost entirely with an isolated
self-examination of conscience; now I think it should
be also concerned with a contemplative survey of everything that has gone before. This is what Karl Rahner
means by the connection between the eucharistic cult
and the "Mass of Life". "The silly phrase," he writes,

"that people use about worshipping better under the blue dome of heaven than at Mass has a kernel of genuine truth; . . . The 'Mass of Life' is a necessary condition for the 'Mass of the Church'."

In the divine office too we must get back to the old emphasis of short, sharp, corporate and objective praise, ruthlessly eliminating all other aspects. Without this straightforward orthodox approach, the divine office does not make sense. But we might add the traditional secondary emphases in which the morning office presupposes the praise of God Almighty by the Church, for, on behalf of, and in the whole creation. Mattins is the Church's recapitulation of the praise of all creatures after their kind; it is the articulation of the glory given to God by the animal and vegetable kingdoms. Likewise the evening office stresses redemption but also, in an Irenaean way, the redemption of all things recapitulated in the incarnate redeemer. These emphases are Benedictine, and I think they are also contemporary. Here is not only the necessary theological complement to a this-worldly *attrait*, but something which truly links this world with the realms of glory, which synthesises immanence and transcendence. It should be unnecessary to add—but the unpleasant truth must be faced—that what goes on in our churches under the head of morning and evening prayer is often theologically indefensible and, to the instinctive outlook of modern people, utterly meaningless. But our need is not for new services: it is for old offices. Theological *usage* makes this quite clear.

We may now safely consider the difficult question of private prayer within this context of the use of theology by and for twentieth-century Christian people. It is only this threefold pattern of formal prayer, be it remembered, which creates the Christian recollective state described in the last chapter. We have put things the wrong way round only in order to try to discover how the product is related to the process; how the specifically modern product might rebound and assist the process.

Although what is here meant by prayer is wider than the conventional meaning there is also a sense in which the word is used in a narrower way: we are only concerned with prayer as the mediator between theology and Christian life, as a way of using theology. This is in no way meant to detract from the simple, traditional, non-theological (but not un-theological) types of prayer which are here omitted. Petition, intercession, thanksgiving and confession retain their proper places.

The first modern need, then, is a way of prayer whereby straight theology becomes "absorbed" into the depths of the personality. The questions to which answers are sought in discursive meditation are "What does this mean?" and "What does it require of me?" The question which modern people seek by contemplative absorption is rather "Whas does this fact do to my existence?" It may be argued, as indeed I have argued myself, that the second meditative question comprises an existential, active response or kerygmatic encounter with the Word of God. The difficulty, however, in down-to-earth pastoral terms, is that it seldom works like that. It is comparatively rare for an arbitrarily selected passage of Scripture to lead to a plain command from God to the man at prayer, and there is no obvious reason why it should. With the proviso that a newly converted Christian lays the foundation of life by contemplating the basic straight truths of the creeds, the first rule towards a modern spirituality is that the subject matter of prayer must *not* be of arbitrary selection. It must begin in the world as response to an existential situation. We are inclined to belittle those devotional manuals which give a list of human needs and troubles with another neat list of biblical passages that are supposed to deal with them. No doubt this is an ingenuous approach to biblical studies, and indeed to prayer, but at least it has the advantage of beginning at the right end. Prayer can hardly be virile if it is divorced from experience, and a long list of subjects and passages to be prayed over a period is that sort of unnecessary discipline against which modern man rebels.

If the straight list of biblical passages is over-simple, how then are the subjects of prayer to be selected in accordance with practical needs? The answer must be by pastoral theological hunches. The well-trained Christian may be led to his own intuitive selection from doctrine, but if this fails it is a matter for spiritual guidance. And this is where pastoral theology enters into the realm of applied or ascetical theology: the application of a general wide sweep of pastoral knowledge to the needs of an individual person in a particular situation. In normal spiritual guidance this is, in fact, what *begins* to happen. A situation is discussed at a personal level and the spiritual guide (priest *or* layman, do not forget) tries to think of some aspect of Christian truth which throws light on the matter. Thus the conversation develops. He who is guided may express thanks for enlightenment, the thoughts of the guide have been helpful, but he departs with little more than theories. He has learned something new about the Christian revelation; it might constitute straight theology which spontaneously changes his life, but this will be rare. The new doctrine needs to be pin-pointed and then absorbed, otherwise the usefulness of the guide's counsel will be short-lived. Exactly how is this to be done?

A pastoral hunch leads us to look firstly to St. Thomas Aquinas for two reasons. He would appear to be favour-able to our rather lax use of the idea of "contemplation" as distinguishing between discursive thought and a simple, comprehensive *look* at an object and thus the quest for a harmony with it, or absorption of it. St. Thomas also sees a relation between discursive thought and contemplation which is far less rigid than we have come to associate with post-Reformation schemata. With a current reaction against rigidity of definition in spiritual thought, St. Thomas becomes curiously up to date. And St. Thomas has a good deal to say about the contemplation of *truth* as such, but this is not an academic exercise. Following St. Anselm, the contemplation of truth is directed to a greater knowledge of God and a greater realisation of the facts of the Christian revelation: the intellectual solution of problems is secondary. We are well out of the "Q.E.D. complex".

Now it is notoriously difficult to "teach" contemplation of this elementary type, but St. Thomas, and those who follow in his tradition, give us a fairly clear view of its development. Reduced to its simplest pastoral level, the teaching of the *Summa Theologica* (II, II, Q. 180, iii) suggests four steps: *reading*, "reception of principles"; *meditation*, "deducing from the principles, the truth the knowledge of which is sought"; *prayer;* and then *contemplation*. If this sounds a little frightening, and the sort of "method" to which modern people are not attracted, I think it can be simplified and, as it were, pastoralised.

Reading and *meditation* mean the following up of a pastoral hunch, and this is initiated by spiritual guidance; by talking the thing over and reducing it to *the* doctrine applicable to the circumstances. This is followed by literally reading, thinking about, meditating upon this doctrine until it becomes quite clear and reduced to a single relevant doctrinal fact. *Prayer* to St. Thomas means the response to grace and is therefore applicable to the total sacramental life of the Christian in which this contemplative exercise and all else is set.

This single truth can now, and only now, be contemplated, absorbed into the personality: "inwardly digested" as the Advent collect puts it. This truth should be taken into silence and solitude (the technique of making retreats, and especially of delivering retreat addresses, is of much importance here) and calmly, simply looked at for a reasonable time. It should *not* be a continuation of reading and meditation, it should *not* be a consciously discursive exercise, but the contemplative consummation of it. Some spiritual writers teach a method of continuous ejaculation of some simple formula—"God in Love", "God is a Trinity", "I am 'in Christ' ", slowly and at intervals over a period. Perhaps this sort of technique is useful to some. But with the serious Christian, even the serious beginner, in mind, I do not think this exercise of absorption should be unduly difficult. Perhaps Cardinal Lecaro sums it up as well as anyone: "It is, indeed, quite natural that once the human mind has gained possession of the truth after much labour in reasoning and analysis, it should rest in the calmer activity of synthesis, of admiration, and, as it were, of savouring. Grace does not destroy nature but perfects it; why then should not this further and higher stage be open to us, in our relation to supernatural truths which have already been thoroughly investigated by the exercise of meditation?" (*Methods of Mental Prayer*, p. 150.)

As all spiritual authors agree, the final act of contemplation cannot be reduced to a "method", but the following points might be added. First, the modern Christian, who is not attracted by "methods" anyway, should be encouraged to give time to this attempt at the contemplation, or absorption, of divine truth. He should be told very plainly that time thus given *cannot be wasted* since it is a disciplined response to grace. Distractions are inevitable, and perseverance is required, so is bold experiment.

Secondly, Lecaro's summary has plain associations with

the Sabbath tradition in spiritual theology: first the active work of the mind, then the loving contemplation of its fruits. It is here that I think the recollective ascetical disciplines in life—the contemplation of the garden, the do-it-yourself at home—will assist the formal contemplation of truth.

Thirdly, rather than imposing some difficult scheme on modern Christians, we are but assisting and utilising their rediscovery of theological interest. Without this kind of guidance in the use of theology and its consummation in contemplation, we are back to the impoverished idea of "instructed Christians"; those with a modicum of knowledge about their faith which offers no constructive guidance to life. We are also bound to end up with a body of Christians who are not only instructed but extremely bewildered. Even if the modern Christian is weaned away from the old "Q.E.D. complex", if he realises that every book he reads is not going to finish with a list of neat conclusions with which every other book is going to agree, he is still liable to become bemused by a tangle of ideas, contradictions and theories. If, moreover, he lacks the foundation of the contemplatively absorbed facts of the creeds, the continued reading of theology, especially modern theology, is probably going to weaken rather than strengthen his faith. This is why those who are merely instructed in the basic verities, who merely "hold" the creeds, who give then an intellectual assent, are severely shaken by contemporary radical speculation. Those who have absorbed the faith by prayer, on the other hand, are invigorated and inspired by it.

Fourthly, although the divine office is of supreme value irrespective of any side effects, its correct recitation forms an exercise in contemplation of this elementary type. The offering of the office to God, with the mind firmly fixed on God alone and a disciplined refusal to be drawn into subjective and discursive cogitation, is a contemplative technique. Habitual recitation tends to assist the practice of simple contemplative prayer.

Fifthly, the contemplation of creatures, of things, is an important step towards the contemplation, thence absorption, of intellectual truth. A disciplined attention directed towards a crucifix—or a daffodil or anything else—is also a value in its own right. It is the establishment of an I-Thou relation with creation, and through it with God, but it is also a total discipline of mind, will, love and senses which leads naturally to the contemplation of the revealed truths of Christian doctrine. From this point, parables and even paradoxes become creative through contemplation. The central truth of Chalcedon—"two natures in one person, distinct yet indivisible"—is an inspired paradox which is only consummated, absorbed, "seen", truly understood and rendered usable, by the contemplation of the living presence of Christ. And an intermediate step towards this may well be the contemplation of a crucifix

In his brilliant, if not too easy book about contemplation, Hans Urs von Balthasar says: "This looking to God is contemplation . . . It is an unwavering 'gaze', where 'looking' is always 'hearing' . . . This gaze, this 'looking' is directed towards the perfect fulfilment promised to created nature in its entirety." (*Prayer*, pp. 20–21.) But only the pure in heart can see God. Contemplation is progressive, and so divisible into an infinite series of degrees. In ordinary pastoral life we have to develop our capacity from the beginning, from the "first form", thus the "unwavering gaze", the "looking" and "hearing" is applicable to a heirarchy of value: from the contemplation of things, to divine truth, ultimately to God himself. This is why and how the whole Christian life is directed towards the final goal; the office, the eucharist, the moral struggle and ascetical disciplines all, in their way, lead to it.

Such a wide purview is necessary if the new-found interest in theology is not to end in frustration. Only by seeing the simple contemplation of truth, whether dogmatic or expressed in paradox and parable, as the immediate consummation of reading, can Anglicans safeguard their essential freedom without being bogged down in a mass of contradiction and dispute. No one wishes to curb or regiment this exciting new concern for theological study. Personal responsibility, of which theological interest is a fruit, insists on complete freedom of choice: there can be no Anglican *Index*. Nevertheless I think a majority of Anglicans would welcome some guidance; guidance not on what they should read so much as on how to make their own personal choice more responsibly. And I think my tentative scheme of contemplative absorption does just that. It suggests that, having been grounded in the straight facts of the faith, and continuing the personal struggle in prayer seen as the guide to life, the right subject to be studied will arise out of the existential situation. The pastoral hunch, intuited by the person concerned or suggested by guidance, will suggest a line of reading from both ancient and modern writers. So the subject-matter of the books read will be dictated by experience, not by an artificial syllabus. This will lead to the possibility, not necessarily of a Q.E.D. solution to the problem but at least to a personal hypothesis, or even a paradox, which can be made subject to contemplation. Such a scheme has the considerable advantage of saving the busy laity from trying to read too much, and what little they do read is related to practical life from the start. Thus pastoral theology in this context begins not with the question: "Here is a book; is it 'relevant' to modern life?" but with "Here is an aspiration (not necessarily a 'problem') within *my* (or perhaps *our*) Christian life; how does theology solve or fulfil it?"

An objection will arise at this point, if it has not arisen in the reader's mind before. We have been discussing prayer, and we have been thinking of prayer in terms of Christian life according to the revealed word of God. We have talked of books, patristic, medieval and modern: should not all this have something to do with the Bible, especially in so far as it has become more and more central to current spiritual theology itself?

The answer is to look again at what we have been doing. Briefly: we began with an experience or situation in life, then allowed a pastoral hunch to lead us into the study of a particular doctrine. The selected books would have doubtless contained a certain amount of biblical reference. This study and meditation was finally crystallised into a single idea, fact, hypothesis or paradox. Now this final glimpse of a simple, supernatural truth may very well be formulated as a biblical text, and it is this portion of the word of God which is to be contemplated and absorbed into the personality. What we have done is analogous to constructing a sermon the wrong way round. The wrong way round, that is, from the scholar's point of view but, according to my previous distinction of the two disciplines, I think this is the right way round from the pastoral theological point of view.

The "scholarly" sermon, or meditation for that matter, starts with a selected biblical text or passage. In modern studies this would be placed in its wider context of historical and critical background knowledge and there would be reference and cross-reference to other biblical passages. But the purpose is to draw out the fullest meaning of the selected text and then, if possible, to show its relevance to Christian life in a general way. Everyone who has listened to sermons or made meditations knows that this is an extremely difficult matter, and however hard the preacher tries the relevance of his text is often overstrained or non-existent, or his teaching remains on the academic level. It did, after all, take the whole Church several centuries to produce credal and dogmatic formulae out of its concerted study and meditation on the scriptures. It is asking a great deal of preacher or layman at prayer to arrive at the same orthodox conclusions in a few hours. In any case he cannot approach the Bible without a previous knowledge of, and faith in, the creeds. And should not the creeds, this final crystallisation of the faith and experience of the whole Church be *used*? If we must always *begin* with the Bible we are back with the scholar's "original source" paradox: what is the point of writing commentaries or formulating creeds if the idolatry of "original sources" forbid their practical use? What is the point of commentary or creed if there is no recognised discipline of pastoral theology?

It has to be admitted that, whatever we believe about inspiration and authority, the Bible does not automatically pulsate with life. The devout layman today, dutifully re-reading the familiar narrative, is seldom inspired spontaneously. He has to work extremely hard to render the text into kerygmatic or existential meaning so long as he keeps to the "scholarly" order: Bible-creed-life. If he starts the other way round: existential situation—hunch —doctrine—contemplative absorption—Bible, then the text into which his studies and prayer has crystallised is alive just as soon as he reaches it. And it is alive because it has grown out of life; there is no artificiality created by intellectual or imaginative gymnastics. The text *is* relevant, it has not been *made* relevant.

We have yet to face the outstanding problem of modern spirituality: the twentieth-century Christian's idea or image or conception of the person of the living Christ with whom he is confronted, in whom he dwells and who indwells him. The old "three-point" meditation is inadequate and yet there is tremendous value in something like it as a safeguard against Apollinarian errors. A further insurmountable difficulty with the "three-point" method is that, by and large, modern people cannot do it. It is an indisputable pastoral fact that when a guild or fraternity of lay Christians embrace a traditional rule of prayer, it is meditation—generally assumed to mean the "three-point" method—on which the large majority consistently fail. It is a fundamental principle of ascetical theology that when a rule is consistently broken by a body of sincere Christians, it is the *rule* itself that is at fault.

In chapter six I concluded that, in view of this, and accepting the complete lack of physical description of our Lord in the New Testament, the meditative image, though legitimate and of use to a minority, could not be *necessary*. I further suggested that regula issuing in the recollective vision of Christ in people, supported by absorbed Christology, might prove sufficient to guard against Apollinarian error. But the question remains: is there a possibility of another technique of formal prayer which could support and enliven the idea of seeing the sacred humanity manifested in people? I have no clear-cut answer; I am unable to invent a new method of meditation. I can only offer some tentative suggestions which might prove worthy of experiment.

Jesus Christ manifests himself in and through his disciples. That is the burden of a modern outlook which aspires to live the Christian life in the world and which is happier with recollection than with formal prayer; even if it recognises the necessity of the latter. But it is particularly unhappy with meditation of the "three-point" type because it seems divorced from the world of real people, and, even if some image of the person of Christ is attained in this prayer, it carries an aura of artificiality. Can the recollective image of Christ in living people— that is particular living people—be carried over into formal prayer?

The immediate difficulty is that, however Christ truly lives in Tom or Dick, however much their humanity partakes of the sacred humanity of Christ through their sacramental lives, in fact however saintly Tom or Dick may be, to meditate on their image as if it were Christ himself is almost blasphemous. The idea behind the "three-point" meditation, the idea behind the best of Christian painting and sculpture, is that it depicts Jesus as Jesus, as a person different from any other person. The traditional, or for that matter untraditional, portrait of Jesus claims to be the fruit of devout imagination alone. Apart from rare examples like the faithful simplicity of Oberammergau, I doubt if any actor is really happy about portraying our Lord, and an artist would hesitate to paint him exactly from a chosen model. Whether or not this is a correct attitude or whether it is veiled Apollinarianism is beside the point.

Modern Christians who find difficulty in forming such an image cannot substitute the image of Tom or Dick and say that is Jesus, or that Jesus is like that. Now there is a misconception here which is of importance both to this point and to the next one. The idea of a "pure image" of Jesus, in St. Bernard's sense a "carnal" confrontation with his divine person, is either impossible or it is the fruit of an advanced contemplative gift. In other words it is impossible for most of us who do not happen to be mystics, and if we attain to an image in prayer it is in fact based on a known person, or on a composite image of known persons because "what is in the mind was first in the senses". Whether our piety likes it or not any conception of the person of Jesus we have is based somehow on our knowledge of human people. The reason for this devotional discomfort is not Apollinarianism; we are not evading, but trying to express the truth of our Lord's perfect humanity. It is the word "perfect" that causes the difficulty: the humanity of Christ is perfect and sinless whereas all our human acquaintances are imperfect and sinful: how can honest devotion compare the one with the other? Ultimately it cannot because imperfection cannot conceive of perfection, and yet, by the doctrine of analogy, this is the only way in which we can get an inspired glimpse of the person of Christ in prayer and life.

Our intent, be it remembered, is not to invent a new sort of prayer for its own sake, still less for the sake of being up to date, but to bring into a total Christian life the essential element of devotion to the sacred humanity. We are led to conclude, therefore, that the search for this necessary image or conception of the person of Jesus in modern spirituality should be coupled not with meditation but with intercession. One then thinks of Jesus as in Tom and Dick, but this is no longer an impious comparison; it is but the use of a theological fact. Christ is in Tom and Dick because of their baptism, or because of their recapitulation within Christ the second Adam. Where they truly, if partially, manifest the qualities of Jesus, then our formal prayer leads into thanksgiving. When their sin, or trouble, or problem tends to obscure the presence of Christ in their life and being, then we are led into an extremely efficacious type of intercession. We thus truly glimpse the sacred humanity in the humanity of Tom and Dick; positively when grace prevails in them, negatively by an analogous glimpse of Christ's perfection as it stands out in contrast to their sin and frailty. Thus intercession, as well as contemplation and study, begins firmly in the world: it is a living personal relationship with Tom and Dick which inspires both intercession and a devotional approach to the sacred humanity. This in no way detracts from the wider duties of intercession for other people, groups and societies on a less personal basis. In fact such personal and from-the-world intercession for Tom and Dick may very well inspire and revitalise the wider intercessory duty.

Exactly the same reasoning is applicable to petition and penitence. To accept, absorb and use the theology of baptism, recapitulation and sacramental grace means to look into oneself in the same way as we have looked at Tom and Dick. Any achievement that grace has wrought in oneself is both cause for thanksgiving and a living relation, a confrontation, between oneself and the person of Christ. Conversely, if at first sight it appears blasphemous to make any comparison between the humanity of Tom and that of Jesus, how much worse to think of the sacred humanity in comparison with one's own. But this is precisely what the Church counsels, and always has counselled, as the very foundation of penitence. And penitence is more than sorrow: it is another glimpse of the person of Jesus manifested in the analogous gulf fixed between his perfection and my sin. And it is closely allied to Christian hope, and therefore to Christian joy. Penitence rightly leads to a hopeful glimpse of what, in Christ, our own humanity will one day be: risen, glorified, Christ all in all.

I do not claim to have solved the problem, but I think there is here some hope that, through a continuing struggle and experiment in the use of theology in prayer, we might have got rid of the "three-point" meditation which modern people find difficult and unattractive. At the same time I think there is considerable hope that intercession, petition and penitence after this pattern, will

I

prove all that is necessary to safeguard the Christological truth.

Am I in time to forestall the obvious query? What about the Bible! It is the same question as before and I think it can be met with the same answer. It is no derogation of the Bible to change its place in the formal making of prayer and I would again put the Bible at the end of the process rather than at the beginning. This does not mean that the scriptures take last place in order of importance but that they consummate instead of initiate our vision of the person of Christ. If a man comes home from his work, eats his meal, and then starts to read the Bible, the living Jesus does *not* spontaneously appear from its pages: it is much more likely that the whole thing will seem quite unrelated to experience, obscure, archaic and dull. But if he thinks about Tom and Dick in an intercessory way, if he couples this with his recollective Christian experience and sees its consummation in his next act of holy communion, if he dwells a little on the living, experiential relation between the sacred humanity and Tom's and Dick's and his own, then I think the matter will be different. He may be reminded of a particular part of the gospel narrative which, like the texts of our previous example, will be alive before he gets to them. In the former instance the seemingly dead text has to be revived by a sort of devotional artificial respiration; in the latter case the life of Tom and Dick are already there. And so is the *life* of Christ for it has been at work, manifesting itself throughout the day. In a devotional vacuum, the New Testament tells us little about the person of our Lord; in this living intercessory situation, in men's relation with Jesus whether by grace, by petition or by penitence, things are different. It is by this devout and penitential comparison that the character of Jesus, the perfection of his humanity and the glory of his love, really shine forth.

The story of Magdalene only lives when we meet and know and love a Magdalene, and then, when we next meet her it will be Christ that shines forth. Without the New Testament all this would be impossible, and without the enveloping context of prayer and recollection, "seeing Christ in people" degenerates into a sentimental delusion.

This point, however, leads on to further consideration of what is, from the spiritual theological point of view, the central aspect of modern biblical studies. How is this biblical theology to be used? How does it function?

CHAPTER TEN

The "Historical Jesus"

Practical Christian discipleship consists in a response to the person of Christ. This is prayer which theology guides and which issues in action. All theology may be found usable for this primary guidance, yet faith in and response to credal statements, saving events, proclamation, are only secondary aids in our response to the person of Christ. And the *kerygma* comes into this secondary category. Whatever the difficulty of biblical language, especially mythological language, whatever the relation between kerygma and the message of Jesus, and however valuable the concept of kerygmatic preaching may be, in the last resort the kerygma is not a person, any more than the Chalcedonian Definition or the Nicene Creed is a person. Protestant spirituality as represented by scholars like Friedrich Heiler and H. H. Farmer is therefore correct in placing *colloquy* at the centre of Christian prayer, even if they fail to see contemplative union and adoration as its peak. For colloquy means dialogue between man and God manifested in Christ: the original, existential confrontation.

Rightly understood, colloquy demands the use and guidance of the whole creed. Dialogue with God, in Christ, by the Holy Spirit, implies the use of the doctrine of the Holy Trinity. Confrontation with Jesus demands Christology, and such dialogue, if it is real and honest, must contain a large penitential element, and so it pre-

supposes some idea of atonement. And all Christian
prayer, even the most personal, is set within the context
of the doctrine of the Church. But, essential as the creed
is, it is still not a person, and you cannot have a conversation with a creed—or with the kerygma. With whom
then do we enter into dialogue, with whom do we converse, hold colloquy? Only with the risen, glorified and
ever-present Christ. Some clear conception of Christ as
person seems absolutely necessary at the very centre of
Christian living. How is this brought about? From the
viewpoint of biblical theology it introduces the problem
of the "historical Jesus". But in order to understand and
use this theology in the context of modern prayer, we
should start by employing the pastoral theological technique of placing the problem in a wider setting: within
the broad sweep of Christian history. The question then
becomes how has this initial confrontation with Jesus
been brought about in past Christian experience? Such
a broad sweep over Christian history might uncover a
usable hunch.

The New Testament gives no hint at all towards an
image of the person of Jesus, therefore such cannot be of
necessity. And this would appear to have been the view of
the Church for over a thousand years: the problem did
not arise. The overwhelming Easter experience, the
known and felt fact of life in the resurrected Christ simply
continued. Even the so-called dark ages were dark in so
far as the gospel was overridden by barbarian conquest
yet the monastic pockets of Christianity were full of light.
Nevertheless it is not difficult to imagine that, after a
thousand years, the overwhelming reality of the Easter
experience might wear a little thin. That the evangelists
saw no need for descriptions of the person of the risen
Lord means that they cannot have been necessary, but it
does not rule out the possibility that, in other ages, such

an image became more useful and significant. The revival of devotion to the sacred humanity, and the approach to Christian living in terms of a loving relation with Christ as person was the tremendous achievement of St. Bernard of Clairvaux.

In characteristic, down-to-earth fashion, St. Bernard spoke bluntly about what he called "carnal" affection for Jesus, and this had repercussions in practically every school of medieval spirituality. Of particular significance in following our pastoral hunch is that it gave rise to what might be called the first series of devotional Lives of Christ, as well as more doctrinal meditations which nevertheless contained a good deal of imaginative biographical description. Most of these came from the great flowering of affective devotion in the fourteenth century: the Pseudo-Bonaventure, Ludolf the Carthusian, and that galaxy of women mystics like St. Gertrude, St. Bridget, St. Catherine of Siena and Julian of Norwich.

Reformation spirituality was, by and large, either a modified continuation of this tradition, or a return to the primitive, pre-Bernardine emphasis on liturgy and formal prayer. In ascetical-theological terms it was a return to speculative prayer in reaction to some of the medieval excesses of affective devotion. The Counter-Reformation, rightly so-called in terms of spiritual theology, was a return to St. Bernard, and it saw the rise of that systematic meditation on the person of Jesus typified by the systems of St. Ignatius Loyola and St. Pedro of Alcantara. Here the free use of the imagination in devout approach to the sacred humanity was encouraged: the three-point meditation came into being. It is hardly surprising that from this movement what I shall call the second series of devotional Lives of Christ arose, a great many from Spanish Jesuit sources: Louis of Grenada, Luis of La Palma, Nicolas Avancini.

It was to this type of prayer that the pastoral side of the Oxford Movement appealed. Thus there arose, particularly in Anglicanism, the third series of Lives of Christ of which the best known exemplar is Dean Farrar. It is significant that the majority of these devotional studies came from the Tractarians who were attracted to the three-point meditation, and also that this devotional movement ran parallel with the original "quest for the historical Jesus" in biblical scholarship.

At the beginning of the twentieth century, this quest came to an abrupt and violent end. And I think it says something for my fundamental hypothesis that, although the three-point meditation continued to be taught (and in isolated pockets of old-fashioned Tractarianism continues to be taught today) its decline starts at this point. Whether or not this kind of prayer was ever successfully practised by Anglicans is debatable; the plain moral remains that devotional method is doomed to failure when it runs counter to contemporary scholarship, however far apart the two appear to be.

It is for these reasons—the pastoral hunches arising out of this broad survey of devotional development—that I have watched the current movement of biblical studies known as the "new quest for the historical Jesus". The last thing I should ever claim to be is a biblical scholar, but there seemed cause for hope that the scholars might unearth some new approach to the gospel narrative which could revivify modern devotion after the Bernardine tradition. So far, however, these hopes have not been realised. In spite of the deep spirituality inherent in modern scholarship, the new quest remains on an entirely academic level. Nevertheless, in the setting of our pastoral wide sweep this negative result is not without interest and it need not be without use.

James M. Robinson points out that the "historical

Jesus" is a technical phrase of which the adjective is neither vague nor superfluous (*A New Quest of The Historical Jesus*, p. 26): "Consequently the expression 'historical Jesus' comes to mean: 'What can be known of Jesus of Nazareth by means of the scientific methods of the historian?' " In our present discussion this means two significant things. First, that although the new quest is not entirely negative in that, as Bornkamm has shown, the gospels tell us more about Jesus than Bultmann or Schweitzer allow, "No one is any longer in the position to write a life of Jesus." (*Jesus of Nazareth*, p. 13.) This means that there is insufficient *historical* evidence in the New Testament. If, therefore, Christians are to gain any real relation with the living and glorified Christ, their prayer cannot *begin* with the Bible. Any real conception of the person of Christ in daily life cannot be *grounded* on historical evidence. This does not deny that Jesus was an historical person, or that the Christian faith is based on historical events, or that the Bible says nothing about him as person. It points to the fact that there is more than one source of religious truth, and that we must seek our Lord in something other than technical history. To this we shall return in a moment.

The second point is that there can be no historical Jesus in the nineteenth-century sense of one divorced from later doctrinal implications. There can be no "simple faith" as of following our redeemer "without being cluttered up with dogma and ritual." And as I tried to explain earlier, "confrontation with Jesus Christ" is an infinitely richer conception than the Protestant and individualistic "acceptance of Jesus as personal saviour". From the point of view of spirituality this is precisely what is to be expected. Although it is another "negative" aspect of biblical scholarship, it gives positive support to that orthodoxy which insists that "private devotion", whether biblical meditation or some other kind, cannot be divorced from the total regula: biblical devotion is impossible without eucharistic experience and our experience of Christ is indissociable from the experience of the Church. It would appear that modern biblical scholarship in the form of the new quest, though largely disappointing from this particular viewpoint, nevertheless supports my tentative suggestion that our knowledge of the person of Christ today must spring from a complex of sources: from our experience of Christ in other people, from intercession, from eucharistic worship, from colloquy, and *finally* from the gospels. It cannot arise solely from the first of the three-points of Ignatian-type meditation. The main problem is still unsolved, can we go further in our search for some devotional introduction to the person of Christ?

Following our wide pastoral sweep of history it is unlikely that we can ever recapture the vivid sense of the presence of Jesus as depicted in the Lives of Christ of the seventeenth-century Spanish or nineteenth-century English or French traditions; that is of our "second or third series". Because these *Lives* were imaginative and not historical does not necessarily condemn their devotional value: history is not the only source of religious truth. It is because these run counter to current biblical scholarship that they are unworkable; not because they are wrong but because to modern people they seem artificial and suspect. However ignorant of technical scholarship a Christian may be, there is a subtle relationship within the total economy of the body of Christ which makes him suspicious and aware of conflict. The second and third series of Lives were acceptable to their generations, so was the three-point meditation. To the present generation they are of dubious value.

The question resolves itself into a straight alternative:

can we recapture the vision of the person of our Lord as it manifested itself to the pre-Bernardine Church, *or* to the post-Bernardine mystics of the fourteenth century? The first alternative is in line with current biblical studies: Bultmann is not generally associated with Catholic spirituality but is not this pre-Bernardine vision precisely what he is trying to achieve? As I understand his position, he is anxious to get rid of images, symbols and myths which surround the image of Christ in the gospels and return to the experience of the original Easter-event; the experience of the risen and glorified saviour which was so overwhelmingly real that any forced methods and techniques of prayer were superfluous. Is not kerygmatic preaching aimed at reproducing this experience? Is not Bultmann's plea to get rid of an artificial devotion to the Jesus of history in favour of an existential acceptance of saving faith in the great events of his life, in the fruits of Christ's redemption?

This is modern biblical scholarship in tune with the contemporary spiritual mood, but is it a genuine possibility in terms of the basic Christian accent of faith in a person? The kerygma is not a person, but can it give rise to that overwhelming experience of the Christ-event which characterised the first millennium of the Church's existence? It must be asked with the most sincere respect how often, and in how many cases, Dr. Bultmann's own sermons have produced this result? My guess at the answer is "sometimes", and that the recapture of the over-whelmingly real but "imageless" sense of the presence of Christ is still possible. But I doubt if it can be regarded as a generally satisfactory ascetical approach to modern prayer. If, after a thousand years, divine providence raised up St. Bernard as a necessary prophet, how much more necessary is his message after another millennium? Once the modern Christian has advanced beyond moralism, and beyond the first flush of religious experience associated with "babes in Christ", some image, or symbol, or conception of the risen Lord becomes a need and a problem. Unless, that is, his conception of God in Christ is not to degenerate into an Apollinarian fog. We either encounter, confront, hold colloquy with *deus-homo*, or we do not.

I conclude that the doctrine of kerygma is not confined to kerygmatic preaching but may play a part in personal prayer, and it cannot be ruled out as a modern technique for some people. But I do not think it is the whole answer.

What of the other alternative? On both biblical and practical grounds the second and third series of Lives of Christ have been ruled out as useless, untheological, and to the Christian man-in-the-street dubious. But what of the first series, the vivid depictions of our Lord in his sacred humanity of the medieval, and especially the fourteenth-century saints? Must all this classic devotion go the way of seventeenth-century Spain and nineteenth-century England? I do not think so.

In terms of biblical scholarship, as a quest for the historical Jesus, it is obvious that the *Revelations* of Julian of Norwich and Dean Farrar's *Life of Christ* come under the same condemnation. They are both unbiblical in that they contain incidents and sayings attributed to our Lord, not to mention Julian's vivid physical description, which are not to be found in the scriptures. They are both unhistorical in that no shred of evidence is forthcoming to support all this extraneous material. If anything Julian comes off worse than Farrar. Yet I am bound to invite the most disciplined, most hard-headed and cold-blooded scholar to make an experiment, and then to offer him a friendly challenge. I invite such a scholar to read these two works in succession, let him bring all his critical faculties to bear upon them both, let him join with me in

condemning them both on the same technical grounds,
then I would ask him: are they works of the same type?
Are they equally artificial and to the ordinary Christian
dubious? Let us rid ourselves of medieval romanticism,
of any semblance of a sentimental regard for antiquity—
which my scholar should not find difficult—and let us
honestly ask: Are these two books rightly destined for the
same dustbin? would you dissuade the ordinary layman
from reading both books on the same grounds? Are they
the *same sort* of rubbish? The answer must be that they are
both unbiblical and unhistorical, but that they are very
different indeed. It has been said, somewhat unkindly,
that Dean Farrar's idea of Christ is that of a typical if
supremely moral Eton and Oxford Victorian gentleman.
If that is unfair there is no doubt that the *Life* is pretty
firmly embedded in the spirit of Dean Farrar's own age
and environment. On the other hand the Christ of the
Revelations bears not the slightest resemblance to a benevo-
lent lord of the manor in fourteenth-century Norfolk, or
to any personification from that particular historical
setting. It must ultimately be a subjective judgement,
literary sensibility varies, yet I think it would be agreed
that if Farrar's portrait is too respectable by half, Julian's
is quite terrifying in its vivid reality. Where lies the real
difference?

The most obvious difference is that, however lightly
he held the reins of disciplined scholarship, Farrar's book
was based on the New Testament. Julian's was not; like
many of her kind she was "unlettered" and the vernacular
text was not available to her. Farrar depended on reason
and imagination, Julian's vision came from prayer flowing
out of a well authenticated mystical experience on May
8th, 1373. With the backing of the total experience of the
Church I have claimed that historical and biblical knowledge are not the only kinds of theological knowledge.

Authentic contemplative experience is equally entitled
to be seen as another part of it. Mystical knowledge is
part of the progressive revelation and like all other
theology—for such it is—it has a primary purpose: a use
and function. This is not obscurantism, superstition,
romanticism or any such thing, and for two reasons.
The fruits of mystical experience have to be tested by
established doctrine, they must stand in the light of revealed truth in conjunction with other aspects of theological knowledge; and if the test is passed the fruits of
mystical revelation must be used correctly. The correct
use of all theological knowledge begins, as I have tried to
explain, with prayer as mediator between theology and
Christian action. The authenticity or otherwise of mystical
experience is judged by the fruits of those Christians who
use it.

Within their fields, therefore, the philosopher, the
biblical scholar and the historian have every right to
question, and to reject, the facts claimed to have been
established by mystical experience. But to leave the matter
there is to limit the range of theology and, ultimately, to
apply the wrong test. Within this present context it is the
failure to distinguish between scholarship and pastoral
theology while recognising their relation. Pastoral theology
again appears as the catalyst which causes reaction between
all the other specialised theologies and makes them usable.

How should a book like Julian's *Revelations* be used?
Certainly not to "prove" anything, still less to create
mystics or teach mystical prayer. The error of the Anglican
1930s was that large numbers of the faithful were led to an
interest in the mystics in the hope that they too might
become mystics, which is just as silly as the current idea
that the sole purpose of scholarship is to produce more
scholars or that poetry is useless if it fails to produce poets.
This is even less sophisticated than straight theology, for

it reduces scholarship to a pale amoeba-like thing whose sole function is to keep on changing its shape. The theological function of Julian of Norwich is not to produce mystics but to present the living Christ to those who never will be mystics. It follows that the three-point meditation might be a fruitful form of prayer for those of marked contemplative gifts—perhaps a majority of the original Jesuits for whom it was intended, but not for the average twentieth-century Anglican. The Anglican's image of Christ is either taken from conventional depictions which are lifeless and unreal, or they suffer even more from Dean Farrar's errors: they partake almost exclusively of the ideas of the present age. Julian's concept is, in the proper technical sense of the word, inspired, so why not use her mystical knowledge to inspire us today? When one looks at the complete range of theological knowledge instead of confining it to the historical and biblical, then Julian, Catharine and Bridget are more advanced than Robinson, Fuchs and Bornkamm: they are also more up to date. As the teaching of St. Irenaeus and Hugh of St. Victor have become current pastoral theology, so too has the vision of the fourteenth-century contemplatives. Their dates are unimportant: they are contemporary because they deal decisively with questions which are contemporary. If pastoral theology is to be up to date it cannot be slave to fashion.

But if Julian's knowledge of Jesus is derived from a contemplative experience and not directly from the New Testament, if it is technically "unbiblical", this does not mean that it is incompatible with the Bible. We have again reversed the order in mental prayer. As the gospel consummates rather than initiates our vision of Christ's humanity in people, in Tom and Dick, so it fills in and consummates those vivid glimpses of the sacred humanity contained in the *Revelations of Divine Love*.

I do not claim to have solved this problem of the image of the person of Christ with whom we are to confront and hold colloquy. But I think our broad sweep over Christian history has at least unearthed one or two extra clues worthy of experiment. Ultimately it is a uniquely personal problem depending for its solution on *attrait* and temperament. Some no doubt can capture the overwhelming presence of the pre-Bernardine Church through response to kerygma, and can honestly dispense with images. Others —I think a very select few—might find the old three points satisfactory and workable. The rest—I think the majority—might get somewhere if they combined a recollective sense of Christ in others with the vision of the fourteenth-century mystics, a combination which would itself enliven the Bible.

This is an important question because of prevalent Apollinarianism and because of the revival of interest in the sacred humanity in current theological studies. Let it be remembered, however, that confrontation with the living Christ is still a wide and complex term extending to Christian experience in Church, society, sacrament and nature.

CHAPTER ELEVEN

A Twentieth-Century Regula?

Skills are notoriously difficult to describe and skilled techniques cannot readily be taught by written direction. Ultimately it all depends on practice and experiment. When the attempt is made to explain skills and techniques in words the unavoidable result is that the whole thing sounds far more complicated than it really is: written, point by point instruction on how to drive a car gives the impression that it is quite beyond the powers of ordinary human beings. It is the same with prayer. Thus the end-product of pastoral theology, and more especially of applied theology, is to reduce theological speculation to the simplest possible framework for action. The ultimate function of theology is to tell us what to do, but if theology first insists that we can do nothing without grace it must first tell us how to respond to grace; in other words how to pray.

By way of summary of our speculations it might be useful to try to state, in the simplest possible terms, exactly what it all boils down to in practice. In view of our quest for a contemporary spirituality it might add to clarity if these results are compared with that spirituality against which modern people rebel. If regula means the traditional system or framework of prayer as the ground of Christian living, which is unchangeable in structure but infinitely variable in detail, how have we adapted the detail in an attempt to serve the modern outlook?

Let us imagine a sincere and intelligent Christian seeking guidance on practical Christian living based on a response to grace through prayer, but first let us imagine his seeking this guidance thirty or forty years ago: what exactly would he be advised to do? If the following is something of a caricature of the spirituality popular in those days, my purpose is only to illustrate the contrast and certainly not to belittle what no doubt served its own age well enough.

First, he would be told that holy communion was the central act of Christian life and that regularity at the altar was his first duty. There would be a great deal about formal preparation, especially by self-examination and fasting. If any positive instruction on eucharistic devotion was given, it would emphasise its "downward" and "forward" aspects: Our Lord comes "down" into the world, and the grace of the sacrament strengthens us to manifest our faith in the world in the future.

Secondly, it is unlikely that any definite teaching about the divine office would be given. If it was the emphasis would be either on duty, without much in the way of ascetical emphasis, or the office would be regarded as a minor "support" to the eucharist without any clear theological function.

Thirdly would come personal devotion, again without any clear connection with liturgical worship. Personal devotion would consist of two distinct things: meditation and vocal prayer. Meditation would certainly be the three-point method, or some close derivative. The subjects of meditation would be defined as a definite and regular programme. It would no doubt be suggested that St. Mark's Gospel was the proper starting point and that this should be worked through story by story and parable by parable. The second part of private devotion would consist in a set period of daily prayer pretty rigidly divided up into the ordinary headings: adoration, self-examination, confession, thanksgiving, petition and intercession.

Fourthly, in general support to this scheme would come an ascetical discipline in life following the traditional pattern: the Friday, Lenten and pre-communion fasts, almsgiving, and perhaps some other little mortifications selected more or less arbitrarily.

Fifthly, spiritual reading would be advised, again more or less haphazardly and without much regard to temperament or specific need.

It would be firmly taught that all this should issue in Christian living, that the moral struggle must continue to the end, and that acts of recollection should be made throughout the day. But the starting point is the sanctuary, the Bible, the spiritual classics.

Now let me hasten to add that there is nothing intrinsically wrong with this pattern, even with certain exaggerations I have permitted myself for the sake of contrast. At first sight it might appear not unattractive even to the modern Christian. If he dislikes too much formalism, this scheme looks reasonably free and it seems to allow a good deal of room for personal choice. But if a modern Christian sincerely tried to carry out such a daily pattern I think he would find it frustrating, fussy, and in the end unworkable and irrelevant. What have I put in its place?

First, the eucharist remains central. But it would begin, not with a long devout preparation, or in the sanctuary, but with Karl Rahner's "Mass of Life". Eucharistic recollection would look forward to the next celebration not back to the last one, yet, at the altar, the emphasis would be reversed. The eucharist would be seen as the consummation of yesterday instead of, or at least as well as, a preparation for tomorrow. Christ indeed comes "down", but the emphasis for today is the Irenaean recapitulation of creation in redemption: all is taken "up" into Christ. Preparation consists of looking at life through the Incarnation.

The divine office, reduced to a traditional, short, workman-like act of praise of Benedictine type comes next. This is absolutely essential if a proper sense of the transcendence of God is to be maintained within a properly world-affirming ascetical sytem. In my hypothetical negotiation with a modern Christian I have said: yes, let us be rid of fussiness and sanctuary-tied pietism; let us begin in the world, let us take our start from the existential situation; but if we are going to do this we simply must counter the terrible danger of subjectivism, immanentism or even humanism. We must recognise the majesty of God outside nature, and the objective offering of the divine office is the well-tried way of doing just that. But, my modern Christian replies, I thought we were getting away from formalism and rigidity, and this is worse than the piety of thirty years ago. Instead of this formal office twice a day, why cannot I just remind myself, by reading or meditation, of the transcendence and majesty of God? I reply: because this is not the only emphasis of the divine office; it also expresses the corporate nature of the body of Christ, it links you with the whole Church, even if you recite it alone. Then why not meditate on the corporate nature of the Church as well as the transcendence of God? To this argument I reply as follows: absorbed theology has to be expressed in prayer or it will not lead to action, continuous meditation on the divine attributes, and on the doctrine of the Church is all very well but it is not *using* theology, it is merely theologising. It is stressing the "academic" which we both want to surpass, while the divine office is action, confrontation, giving, going out to God the Father with one's whole being: is not that what we are trying to do, or are we to be content with just "knowing theology"? And I further reply: do we not want simplicity? a minimum, time and motion framework of prayer which is nevertheless going to be efficient? By the time you have read, and thought, and meditated on the divine glory, and then done that all over again in relation to the doctrine of the organic Church, you will probably have missed your train! Would it not really be easier, simpler and more efficient to learn the technique of the divine office so that all this and more besides is actively done, truly expressed, in five minutes? Are you not writing a long love-letter to send to your wife every day when what she really wants is to be kissed? That would express the situation actively rather better than the laborious letter; and it would be much quicker!

Now comes private prayer. I should suggest the old-fashioned, but necessary discipline of setting aside a daily period of time for formal devotion, and I should leave it severely at that: no three-point meditations to learn and struggle with, no carefully divided bits of time for this that or the other, no pre-selected list of subjects for meditation, intercession, petition and so on. So much time, full stop. Yes, but how is this time to be filled in? Surely there must be some kind of method, technique, skill to be learned? No doubt there is, but I should begin, not with the text-book, or even with the bible, but with existential experience; I should begin to formulate technique in the world. The modern Christian would read a certain amount of theology of a popular kind because theology is now in the air, but this is not "duty" or part of some rigid "rule of life". It is an interest and I should encourage him to go on gently, as he liked and when he liked. This would lead to problems, doubts, wonderings; living issues would arise. I should advise him to take this to a competent pastoral theologian (unless he happens to be one, or until he becomes one himself) and talk about it. This would be an interesting conversation not a profes-

sional interview, and its sole purpose is to produce a
pastoral hunch to follow up. The pastoral theologian is
not there, in this case, to offer counsel or instruction, but
to offer his wide sweep of knowledge in formulating the
hunch. All this implies is an interesting conversation
between a couple of Christian friends over a drink
(alcohol in small doses is rather good for hunches). Then
the hunch is followed up, gently without making a *duty* of
it. Eventually it will resolve into a simple doctrinal fact,
probably crystallised into a biblical text. And this is one
thing to take into formal prayer, to be simply looked at,
contemplated for quite some time until it is absorbed;
until it becomes part of oneself and its implications
spontaneously expressed in life. But how is this done? The
question is a difficult one because the contemplation of
truth is notoriously difficult to "teach". Finally it has to
be just done, practised, experimented with, but if we
stick to the time discipline, even if it is sometimes a little
frustrating and boring I think it gets achieved. Nevertheless
it is considerably helped if we can get into the habit of
the correct offering of the divine office and simplest contemplative activity in daily life, and this grows from the
askesis of aiming at a harmony with an environment. This
in turn comes through something like an I-Thou relation
with things: the garden, the home—"do-it-yourself".

Petition, intercession, thanksgiving, penitence—in fine
colloquy—also come from daily experience: let there be
no regimentation of time or subject, no prearranged
schemes and schedules. This need not rule out intercession
of duty: for the generality of sick and suffering, for the
Church overseas and so on, but there are two good reasons
why this need not be imposed rigidly on the modern
Christian who dislikes rigidity. The radio and newspaper
are very much parts of daily experience and this sort of
intercession will doubtless grow out of them. Of much

more importance is that regula, as primary response to grace within the Church, is in itself the supreme intercessory channel through which God works. Again the simple discipline of the divine office saves a great deal of fussiness: Rule dispenses us from rules. (Might I here add a parenthetic plea that as the Church embraces regula and grows in proficiency, we might hope for some abatement in those dutiful little intercession lists which arrive by every post from every conceivable society, guild and organisation?)

But now the real problem arises: colloquy means converse, dialogue, with a person, and all Christian prayer is offered to God the Father through Jesus Christ. Our modern Christian, if he is honest with himself, will say that the whole concept of the "presence of Christ" is vague and bewildering to him. And if he has any interest in biblical studies he will see that they support him. How, then, does one achieve this introduction to the person of Jesus, how does one "meet" Christ, risen, ascended and glorified? Let us not evade the issue that this is *the* modern problem of which there can be no clear-cut answer. Yet, by way of experiment, I am now in a position to make four suggestions, any of which or any combination of them, might lead our modern Christian into a workable technique. First, there is the attempt to return to primitive Christian spirituality and dispense with symbols and images altogether. Can one not, after all, converse with someone in the dark? Or on the telephone? Is the image essential? No, it cannot be essential for converse is a dialogue of minds and the voice of Christ is heard through human minds because humanity is recapitulated in the sacred humanity. The key to confrontation with Christ may be our own human nature. But this is not at all an easy concept and it might prove unsatisfactory to many people.

Secondly, then, we can look for Christ manifested in others, especially those within the body of Christ: their Christ-like qualities leading into thanksgiving, and their sin into intercession and penitence. Or, thirdly, we could seek inspiration from those with a contemplative vision of the person of our Lord, and—merely by way of suggestion—I think some of the fourteenth-century saints might prove surprisingly up to date. In all these experiments I suggest we consummate our insight by reference to the New Testament narrative. Intercession, petition and colloquy in general will tend to pin-point the stories and passages relevant to the living situation from which they sprang. As a further safeguard against Apollinarian error I would further advise the initial absorption of Christological doctrine.

Fourthly, I should not entirely discount the three-point meditation: a few people will be sufficiently gifted to make use of it, and a few, even modern people, will not be temperamentally antagonised by it. But I should be inclined to advise experiment for a short time, and if, after experiment, frustration and failure appeared to prevail, then give the thing up for good.

Briefly we have remained loyal to the total experience of the Church: the eucharist and the divine office remain the twin pillars of Christian life. But only when their purpose and emphases are also interpreted traditionally. We have got rid of infuriating "duties"; of "going to church" divorced from theological purpose. We have completed the modern regula with so much formal prayer daily, but with no artificial schemes, methods, rules, sub-divisions and all the rest of previous fussiness. Because personal prayer is to spring from living experience, its supporting *askesis* also comes from life and not textbooks. We have also got rid of subsidiary disciplines and "duties" like Bible reading, spiritual reading, fasting dissociated from creative spirituality and study divorced from prayer. And yet none of these things are left out because experience and interest in current, existential factors will bring them in spontaneously.

We have also got rid of the modern Christian's frustration with theology; frustration despite his new-found interest in it. He can read what he likes, following argument and counter-argument, theory and counter-theory, but without the bogey of the "Q.E.D. complex". He can read the die-hard conservative and the radical rebel. Then, instead of a bewildered attempt to "understand" it, he can decide what is sufficiently important, or exciting, to be usable, absorbable, contemplated—and throw the rest away. This is but the retreat technique in which one clings to one point of an address, deemed worthy of personal meditation, without bothering about anything else.

If the layman wishes to go further, if he wants to be a pastoral theologian and a guide to others, if he aspires to what can only properly be meant by a "leading churchman", then he will have to begin at the beginning and follow a course of more systematic studies. And this is only the normal procedure of any personal interest. The expert in fly-fishing, horticulture, music, or anything else most probably began by dipping into the subject somewhere or anywhere. Stimulated interest led him to take the thing more seriously and more systematically, so he became an authority. There seems no valid reason why the same procedure should not apply to theology.

Finally, it is modern theology which has developed the ascetical stress on continuity of Christian living against regularity of devotional acts; which insists that habitual recollection in the world is the end-product of regula. The disciplined response to grace is subservient to the manifestation of faith in daily life, and grace is that unceasing love of God which takes its effect as a long-term process. So, perhaps most important of all, we are rid of that introverted tension which is for ever trying to assess the "results" of individual prayers and spiritual exercises. According to a truly contemporary regula we are no longer concerned with distractions, or wandering thoughts, or whether our meditation is satisfactory, or if this or that prayer is "answered". We make our response full-bloodedly, and then *live*: prayer, as well as theology has suffered too much from the Q.E.D. complex.

CHAPTER TWELVE

The Pastoral Theological Process Examined

By contrast with scholarship our experiment in practical theology began not with texts, manuscripts and sources, but with a serious examination of the modern world with its particular outlook and interest. Insight into such a situation demands the intuition only gained by prayer in the wide sense in which I have tried to describe it. The conclusion of Christian experience throughout history is that such a knowledge of an environment may be gained in either of two ways. It can be gained by direct observation and study, by entering into work and experience of the world itself and by an empathetic relation with people. Or, to the bewilderment of the secular-minded it can be gained by contemplation: the professional religious and the man of unusual holiness usually know more about the world than anyone. The one approach which seems to frustrate the acquisition of this understanding of a social environment is the "in the world and not of it" concept which, in all but the advanced contemplative, is liable to degenerate into being, ascetically speaking, "of the world but not in it". In this context the parish priest finds himself in an inevitable difficulty, but this is less serious when it is remembered that practical theology is not so much the concern of the priesthood as of the organic Church. Whether pastoral theology is produced by priest or layman, the insights of the laity are indispensable, so deeply personal discussion between priest and layman is also indispensable for using theology. Here is a work for Christian lay people of an importance which renders so much current discussion about the place of the laity in the Church quite pathetic. The priest pastoral theologian may be active or contemplative, or a true synthesis of both, but he will not attain the raw material for pastoral theology by hiding behind the parochial group or the clerical collar.

Having gained some insight into the current situation, our next step was to assess its values and dangers. This demanded some knowledge of spiritual theology and the history of spirituality.

The third stage was to look back over, pray back over, meditate, contemplate, think back over, a wide range of Christian history in order to initiate intuitions, links, interrelations and hunches. We started off with three writers from the twelfth and thirteenth centuries, which led us on to two personalist thinkers of the early twentieth century one of which was a Jew. This in turn led us back to St. Irenaeus in the second century. We were then led to consider the relation between meditative prayer and Christology and finished up with current biblical studies in the new quest for the historical Jesus. That, I suggest, covers a wide enough range! It presupposes a fairly comprehensive knowledge of figures, trends, characteristics, emphases and counter-emphases over Christian history. On the other hand a specialised knowledge of any one of these writers need be but minimal. That Hugh of St. Victor constructed a scheme of spirituality based on the symbolic nature of the universe, that St. Francis preached to the birds and wrote the *Canticle*, that Aquinas taught and ordered hierarchy of being, that Buber and Heim were concerned with *I-It* and *I-Thou*, that St. Irenaeus elaborated the doctrine of recapitulation, that there is a movement called the new quest for the historical Jesus: such facts *should* be common knowledge to any first-year divinity student, and they do not approach the lowest rung of the ladder of "scholarship". Such elementary facts however were sufficient to set the pastoral theological ball rolling; they led to a fresh interest in the works in question and began to initiate some constructive pastoral thinking—however inadequate our own results prove to be.

Before the scholar sniggers at this pastoral theological process, before he calls it an insignificant piece of shallow play-acting, so different from his own approach, let him be reminded of two things. First, that the whole point and purpose of this exercise is to bring *his own* work to life for the advancement of Christian people through the medium of prayer. Any help he can give us in interpreting the Fathers, or the Schoolmen, or modern theology, will be gratefully accepted. It is a question of co-operation within the body of Christ.

Secondly, the process under examination has required, if not "scholarship" then at least some modicum of discipline and integrity. The examination of our hunches demanded a ruthlessly objective assessment. If the twelfth and thirteenth-century scholars laid a vague foundation to our thought, it had to be admitted that they did not get us far. St. Francis inspired, suggested, hinted, but he left us very much in the air as to how to use the doctrine unearthed. Heim and Buber suggested themselves at this point, and all these writer pointed to a composite approach to creation which seemed to have something to do with contemplative prayer, with a modern ascetic of environmental harmony. But we were still stuck with the problem of sin, ugliness and evil; the idea of "seeing Christ in people" remained little more than a sentimental idea because so many people seemed to bear little relation

to the Christ we knew by faith. It was only when we were
led back to St. Irenaeus that all this began to make
practical sense. The sentimentality of "God in creation"
gave way to the reality of Christ in creation, manifesting
the redeeming Cross in ugliness and sin as well as in goodness and beauty. Then we arrived at the new quest for the
historical Jesus, inspired by an optimistic hunch that this
body of New Testament scholarship would solve the
problem of the meditative and contemplative image of
Christ. But it did not. Our "inspiration", our intuitive
hunch has led us astray, it was false and had to be aban-
doned. We must try again. Without claiming scholarly
integrity—because we are doing pastoral theology not
scholarship—I do not think this process can justly be
accused of stretching and straining at texts and authorities
in order to justify a preconceived theory. We are not
dealing with theories, but with prayer as the mediator
between theology and modern living, and it has got to
work. In fact it is only on the intellectual plane that prejudice can continue; one can argue with the bigot for
years, but bigotry cannot bear the strain of the usability
of theology in prayer. So prayer rebounds as a valuable
test for the validity of theology.

Although our overall concern is to create pastoral
theology, finally to be applied to individual people, we
might well have unearthed some new straight theology
as well; "new" in the sense of old, academic theology
translated into usable terms within a particular context.
The Irenaeus-Buber-Heim doctrine that all creation is
linked up with the redemption of all things in the resurrected Christ might, if simply absorbed in prayer, spontaneously change the spiritual outlook and experience of
a man pruning his apple-trees. An understanding of the
Franciscan doctrine of poverty could influence a man's
recollective outlook on the world.

Maintaining the doctrine of the organic Church, and seeing the whole of theology as part of its total activity, it should be clear that training in pastoral thinking is by no means the preserve of clergy and candidates for ordination, although they should form a significant group within pastoral theology. It may well be the growing body of theologically concerned lay people who will prove most influential in future pastoral thought, but who may need a little more clarity of approach. If the theological colleges choose to take pastoral theology more seriously as a worthy alternative to pseudo-scholarship, and if my proposals are deemed worthy of consideration, then I shall be gratified, but all that is ancillary to the present purpose.

What happens is that a serious modern Christian interests himself in a popular exposition of the faith, or he might read a controversial book like *Honest to God*. His interest stimulated, he will go on to perhaps Bonhoeffer or Tillich in their more pastoral works. Sooner or later he will find himself reading scholarship and his interest will wane under a jumble of incomprehensible technicalities. The intelligent man is quite prepared for the common experience that the more one knows of a subject the more there is to know; increasing knowledge always shows up one's ignorance. But what he will not realise is that he has unwittingly jumped right out of one subject—pastoral theology—into a completely different, if allied one— theological scholarship. He is like an amateur gardener who, starting with popular journals, finds himself reading a technical treatise on botany. Scholarship is allied to pastoral theology as botany is related to horticulture, but it does not concern the practical gardener. The amateur with a beautiful garden need not feel baffled or frustrated for not knowing botany, nor need the pastoral theologian (clerical or lay) for not understanding technical theology.

The need is for a clear and accepted distinction plus guidance based upon it.

The importance of this new interest in theology is far greater than the comfortable idea of a new generation of "instructed Christians" which is somehow nice to have. *Applied* theology remains the pastoral end-product of the total process, and this implies personal guidance in life through prayer which has ceased to be a priestly preserve. The serious guidance of lay people by lay people is both the cause and outcome of the revivied theological interest, and although ascetical theology—the specific doctrine of Christian prayer—remains a vital part of pastoral theology, the bulk of the doctrine to be personally applied, especially on the more elementary levels, is the basic Christian truth enshrined in the creeds. The patterns of prayer upon which Christian life depends are applications not so much of the categories and techniques of ascetical theology as such—though these will have their eventual place—but of the doctrines of the Trinity, Incarnation, Atonement and of the Church. What then, should constitute a working knowledge of Christian doctrine, a composite course of primary instruction, which should qualify a man—or woman or priest or ordinand—to create pastoral theology? And of equal importance, what should be left out of such a course?

The framework should be a general study of the history of Christian doctrine which itself goes a good way in overcoming that departmentalism of subject matter which has bedevilled theological training for years, and which modern specialisation is liable to accentuate. Within this framework only three interrelated divisions arise, and their relationship should be made a strong element in teaching and approach. These are biblical studies, which link with exposition of the doctrine of the creeds and which give rise to spiritual theology, sub-divided into ascetical and moral theology, including casuistry. All is seen within the general history of doctrinal development. In the case of training for ordination, such a course would keep the average, pastorally-minded student well occupied but not overwhelmed for a three-year period.

The approach to such studies is, however, every bit as important as the syllabus itself, and this approach is qualified by two overall emphases. The first is that pastoral as well as intellectual implications should always be sought. We have noted, for example, how the doctrine of the Holy Trinity expresses itself in the proper emphases of the traditional threefold regula, and how meditation and recollection are embedded in a knowledge of Christology. All too often serious Christians, not omitting ordination candidates, are permitted to recite morning prayer, assist at holy communion, say their private prayers, and read about the doctrine of the Trinity and Incarnation, as if these were five isolated things. The question: "What might this have to do with a concrete situation?" should become an habitual state of mind to the pastoral theological student, while it is not a necessary question for the scholar. What does the doctrine of the Atonement mean to a criminal awaiting execution? What has the Incarnation to do with an apple tree? If St. Anselm is right about the Atonement then however it shocked St. Paul and however it continues to shock devout Christians now, "shall we then sin that grace may abound?" remains a not unintelligent question. If Abelard is right then extreme rigorism in morals and casuistry would appear to be inevitable. In the simplest possible example our prior pastoral question has led us to range over our whole syllabus: creed, Bible, history, spirituality, morals, casuistry.

The second necessary emphasis in approach is the fact of the centrality of prayer. If spirituality is proving a necessity for scholarship, how much more necessary it is for pastoral theology. But as the true centre of studies, not as a pious appendage, for it is only prayer in the sense that we have defined it that can lead to that intuitive quality, that spiritual discernment, which can unearth the hunches at the start of constructive pastoral theology. This point leads into a consideration of what has been omitted from our proposed syllabus.

First, there are no "set books" or "special subjects", no "Introduction to the New Testament", "I Corinthians in Greek", or "The doctrine of Revelation with particular reference to Duns Scotus". And the reason for this is twofold. First, it is pseudo-intellectualism, neither scholarship nor pastoral theology but a worthless hybrid. If scholars produce worthy commentaries from their study of original sources should not these be *used*? Or *are* the Church's scholars making themselves redundant? What exactly is the point of a scholarly exposition of Thomism when every parish priest or layman ought to read the *Summa* anyway? It will be argued, with some point, that even if special subjects and set books add little to a pastoral student's knowledge, they nevertheless give him some valuable training in scholarly method. This still confuses the issue: why should not all the academicians undergo a course in pastoral method? More practically I suggest that whatever weight this argument carries it is an uneconomic use of time for busy lay people or students undergoing a course of less than five years. It is uneconomic because it invariably means that some aspect of the basic pastoral theological framework is going to be left out altogether.

The second point under this first main heading is more important. As soon as the skeleton framework of knowledge is acquired pastoral theology can itself begin to be formulated. As soon as it is capable of giving rise to intuitions and hunches, existential situations will unearth living problems, and this will lead to more specialised studies as the hunches are followed up. The practical doing of pastoral theology will, in other words, lead in to the study of set books and special subjects, but these will be living issues rather than arbitrary selections of academicians setting examination papers. In the example given in the preceding chapters, St. Irenaeus, Heim and Buber, Hugh of St. Victor, the Second Adam doctrine of St. Paul, all arise as "set books", but in context they are concerned with living and exciting problems divorced from what in many cases is but an academic grind. While maintaining the distinction between scholar and pastoral theologian, I do not think that the latter, after this sort of preliminary training and five years' practice, is likely to be an ignoramus: unless that term may properly be applied to Catherine of Siena, Julian of Norwich, Jean Vianney, and other of the Church's "unlettered" saints.

This brings us to the second omission. "Unlettered" means ignorant of Latin, and I have left out all study of languages from my proposed pastoral theological course. The reasons are similar to those given under the first heading. The insistence on languages confuses the needs of the two disciplines. It fails to distinguish between the study of sources and the study of commentaries, and to see that the first is the preserve of the scholar, the second of the pastoral theologian, while both fit into their respective places in the total activity of the body of Christ. The question of the uneconomic use of time given to preliminary training is, however, far more serious here than in the case of set books and special studies. For today, even the would-be scholar finds himself overburdened by the sheer weight of linguistic study required by modern specialisation. There have been times when a competent biblical scholar could get by on Hebrew and Greek;

today he must know German and possibly French. Modern doctrinal studies require not only Latin but German and probably Danish. Spirituality as a definitive subject demands French, Italian and Spanish. Pastoral theology may well be assisted by all of these languages, but it does not demand any. I am thinking, of course, of pastoral theology and not general education. No doubt facility in languages is intellectually beneficial, as a classical education is a proven foundation for any cultural activity. The value of general education applies to anyone, banker, farmer or engineer, but these do not need languages as part of their professional training: the same applies to the pastoral theologian.

I have also omitted a group of subsidiary subjects to be found under the general heading of theological training: liturgy, philosophy of religion, apologetics, and so on. This is not because these are of no importance, but because, with the emphasis on comprehension and synthesis rather than specialisation, they are closely allied with one or other of my three main divisions. Liturgy, especially in the existentialist sense of what a rite is *for* rather than what it is composed of, is a part of spirituality; philosophy and apologetics are allied to both doctrine and pastoral theology as such.

I have finally omitted "pastoralia", including preaching, for several reasons. First, because pastoral and practical theology is no longer the preserve of the priest, whose more special activities may need training of a different kind. In any case I am personally doubtful whether, even in the case of ordinands, "pastoralia" is a proper part of basic theological training. Preaching is largely a question of inherent gifts and experience more than technical training, and I make bold to say that the sermons of anyone taking pastoral theology seriously are unlikely to be deficient in content. Moreover it has to be admitted that, in the modern context of personal guidance through applied theology, and in view of the revived interest in theological studies among the laity, preaching becomes either a part of liturgical studies or an important but comparatively small aspect of the total ministry of the Word.

However inadequate our preceding examples, they constitute only one little piece of pastoral theologising. Confronted with the same situation others would no doubt start in a different place altogether, according to different intuitions. In all probability they would be much more successful. Yet pastoral theology remains the work of the Church, and it is the synthetic results of many experiments which alone can provide an adequate pastoral theological *corpus*. Such a corpus, moreover, would be pastoral theology in the broadest sense; a general body of principles pertaining to such a vague, overall phrase like the "modern world" or the "modern outlook". There will remain an infinite series of more local problems, depending on particular circumstances: environmental, diocesan, parochial and domestic. Finally there will be problems pertinent to unique individual people: the same disciplined principles will apply but we shall have moved to ascetical—applied—theology. Pastoral theology, then, takes on the fashion of an iceberg, the vast bulk of which is hidden and submerged. Only the most general principles will, or can, appear in print, therefore the ability of modern people to *do* pastoral theology, to acquire both the wide background knowledge necessary and the technique involved, is of greater importance than the published works.

Published works, however, have an importance of their own, as examples of pastoral theologising, as the exposition of basic principles, and as a necessary link in the chain between the scholar and the pastor. And because of modern specialisation, pastoral theology has to take on some degree of specialisation itself. Biblical, historical and dogmatic theology all demand their respective pastoral specialists. This also enriches the synthesis of any pastoral theological corpus as well as welding the fruits of specialised scholarship into a creative whole. The biblical, historical or dogmatic pastoral theologian must still start with the existential situation, and after working back through scholarship, he must return to that concrete situation with an hypothesis that can be practically mediated through prayer. He will not, in other words, be a biblical, historical or dogmatic expert with passing pastoral interests; he will be a pastoral theologian whose particular bent happens to be the Bible, or history, or dogmatic theology.

Let us conclude with what must be a cross between a plea and a speculation. Let us endeavour to construct an ecclesiastical situation, set within the contemporary world, in which theology may function as creatively as possible.

CHAPTER THIRTEEN

The Church and the Use of Theology

Unless the Church is to sink still deeper into the bog of expediency, triviality and impotence, it must encourage scholarship in a much more realistic way. Laudatory lip-service to the professional scholar is not enough. The English situation wherein most universities include a theological faculty is healthier than the American system where all theological research is carried out within the Church's seminaries. It is healthier because the study of theology takes its place alongside other disciplines and impinges more closely upon the secular world; the risk of ecclesiastical inbreeding is much reduced. On the other hand the American scholar is obviously working within the Church. In any but the ancient universities of England and Scotland, the priest-scholar is vaguely assumed to have accepted a reputable post of a semi-secular kind: he is somehow outside, or at least not fully inside, the Church itself. And if a scholar with means to support himself decided to live privately, giving his whole time to learning, he would be deemed to have "retired" from the Church's life.

The blame for this attitude cannot be placed all on one side. A distinguished clerical don once asked me what a "rural deanery" was; it was a purely academic question because whatever the answer it was nothing to do with him. On the other side I remember clerical eyebrows raised when a divinity professor in a provincial university was given an honorary canonry: how could such an honour be given to one who had opted out of the "real ministry."

There are three ways of rectifying this position. The first is a greater recognition by both academician and ecclesiastic of the traditional place of scholarship within the total body of Christ. This means that the former should see the end-product of his work as practical Christian life, however long and tortuous the chain of reaction may appear to be. On the other hand the Church, gratefully accepting the service it is offered by the universities, should nevertheless do far more to encourage scholarship within its narrower (ecclesiastical) ranks. If it is no longer possible for parochial clergy to take scholarship seriously, then there is something wrong—in the sense of heretical—with the prevailing pastoral system. Amongst its chain of uses, theology has its *negative* function as a test and safeguard for pastoral practice and parochial organisation. It needs little perception to see that a good deal of what is now regarded as the norm could not stand up to any such test.

The second way of alleviating the position is to place more emphasis on the catalytic agency of prayer. This is no pietistic exhortation to scholars to be more devout, but to follow through their own discovery that spirituality is part and parcel of modern theological studies. Prayer thus becomes not only a catalyst within the theological chain of reaction but also the all-embracing bond of unity between the academic and the ecclesiastical environments.

The third way is something of a synthesis of the first and the second, and it is perhaps the most important. It is the recognition of pastoral theology as a valid discipline of the type I have tried to explain. But this recognition is demanded of both academic and ecclesiastical authority.

I should therefore propose the ideal in which any senior student submitting a higher degree thesis is first asked whether he wishes to be examined under the rules of scholarship or under the rules of pastoral theology; the two disciplines being clearly differentiated. In the former case the student's use of source material, his precise documentation and his ability to follow a logically integrated theme on a narrow front, should go a long way to a pass. Practical implications and startling originality should not be required and could validly be condemned. On the other hand, acceptance of a pastoral-theological thesis would depend on a far-reaching, if more superficial knowledge of several aspects of theology, coupled with original intuitions convincingly worked out. The demand for originality would apply not to new doctrine but to new application. Such work would have to include knowledge of current trends in scholarship, yet I believe it would also inject new life into the study of Patristic, Medieval and historical learning. To study what the Fathers said and meant for the purposes of degree winning is a pretty dull business because it is not what their writings were for, and I dare say most of them would be scandalised at the very idea. To look for what they might possibly have to say to the contemporary situation is an exciting quest.

The acceptance of pastoral theology is equally necessary on the ecclesiastical side. I doubt if it will be particularly profitable to labour the point of the Anglican tradition of learning, and look nostalgically back to the seventeeth century when learned tomes poured out of English country parsonages. A very few modern parish priests are likely to enter the ranks of top class scholarship, not because they are incapable, or even because they are too busy, but because of the high degree of specialisation involved. It is now impossible to keep abreast of any subject without access to a high-class academic library and to a large number of learned journals. My guess is that not a few potentially top rank scholars outside the main academic channel have given up in despair. But they, and a good many others as well, could add valuable contributions to pastoral theology, which, having been reared in the disciplines of scholarship, they regard as third-rate stuff not worth the effort. Yet here, on the ecclesiastical side of the fence, is the obvious location for the pastoral theologian as mediator, *via* prayer, between scholarship and Christian life.

If the pastoral Church—the ecclesiastical side—can encourage and embrace its scholars, instead of relying entirely on the universities, all well and good. But if theology is deemed to have a pastoral function it is difficult to see how any cathedral chapter, group ministry or rural deanery, can be regarded as complete without its own pastoral theologian. For here is the link not only between scholarship and practice but also between pastoral and applied theology. The application of theology *via* prayer to the unique needs of individual Christian people is the last and most vital link in the whole chain. This is the pastor's supreme work, be he clerical or lay, yet it is disastrously neglected.

The knowledge necessary for this ultimate work of spiritual guidance is primarily pastoral theology applied to the creeds and only secondarily the study of ascetical theology strictly so-called. Such knowledge, therefore, cannot be regarded as an optional extra, and theology applied to the needs of persons by spiritual guidance cannot be thrown off as the province of a few specialists. In current practice such guidance is either given with little real competence or, irresponsibility masquerading as humility, the pastor seeks out a "specialist" to do his own proper job. Nevertheless, there is a long road between normal pastoral guidance and the properly specialist experience required to deal with advanced contemplative prayer or unusual *charismata*. The competent pastor will meet many cases along this road; uniquely personal questions which do not warrant the true specialist yet which are sufficiently unusual to be baffling. The obvious procedure would be to consult the local resident pastoral theologian: but first there must be one.

The theological colleges ought to be another medium of communication between the academic and the ecclesiastical; between scholarship and pastoral theology. Regrettably this is not so because the distinction and interrelation is not recognised. Scholarship remains the only norm, in consequence of which the teaching in institutions primarily concerned with the training of *pastors* becomes a most miserable hybrid: pseudo pastoral theology crossed with third-rate scholarship. The syllabus begins with an "introduction to" Biblical studies, Patristics, church history and so on. So far, so good: but then, what looks like the start of a wide pastoral sweep is abruptly narrowed down, scholarshipwise, to set books and special subjects. The ability to translate little texts from St. Augustine and give a minute commentary on them is not of any pastoral use. To understand the basic implications of Pelagianism, Donatism, Manichaeanism, concupiscence, temptation, the Incarnation and the Trinity according to St. Augustine, is knowledge without which no pastor can be competent.

If we kept to pastoral theology proper, eliminating the set books, special subjects, bits and pieces of languages, and so on, our theological colleges would produce two results. They would produce a few pastoral theologians in the sense of those who could construct some of the many books we so badly need in this particularlar form. What is even more important, all future pastors would be able to *do* pastoral theology in the sense of applying scholarship to the unique needs of individual Christians in unique circumstances. And this is the end-product: an ability which cannot be printed, and one without which all the books are futile. To substitute pastoral theology by "pastoralia", to give up theological training in favour of practical know-how, is the supreme disaster and the supreme heresy. It is the purposeful throwing over of the faith once delivered to the saints for something altogether different. It also implies the continuance of a pastoral pattern, and a pastoral outlook, which cannot stand before theological investigation.

With the emerging pastoral pattern, however, practical theology, applied theology, pastoral theology, cannot be restricted to the professional interests of clergymen. This is the revived doctrine of the Church which must include the laity in any new complex of pastoral relationships. It is manifested in the current emphasis on the participation of the laity in administrative government, in liturgical experiment, and in their new-found interest in theological questions. It would be a tragedy, certainly an Anglican tragedy, if this fresh zeal was allowed to stop short of pastoral concern. Current ascetical-theological emphasis also militates against "over-direction" by priests. But this is a subtle movement which, though rightly stressing personal responsibility against authoritarianism, nevertheless rejects not personal guidance but a particular type of it. Christian sociology confirms the Anglican ideal which thinks of a totally integrated Christian community rather than of a priesthood divided from a homogeneous laity. Spiritual guidance by applied theology takes on a more deeply personal character. The relationship involved is no longer one that can adequately be expressed in terms of a priest's "interviews" with "clients". It is much more personal, more of a continuous relation, and far less of a

rigid "counselling". A good deal of modern guidance
takes place round the fireside, or in any other social
environment, and it is plain that the new laity should be
encouraged to guide one another. This brings up the
much discussed question of lay-training, or adult religious
education, or the layman's place in the modern Church.

Let it be said at once that the devout layman, living
within the embrace of regula and putting all his energies
into his family, his hobbies and his job, is perfectly fulfilling
his vocation in the redemptive body of Christ. He need
not read a lot of theology if he does not want to, nor is he
acting irresponsibly by refusing to be a sidesman. But
many more modern laymen, perhaps more especially
laywomen, will be interested in theology and vocationally
attracted towards its applied use in the guidance of others.
We are back to the broad sweep of historical theology
proposed as the frame of theological college curricula. And
this must be the most obvious use of religious education or
parish study group programmes. For here, too, the shadow
of third-rate pseudo-scholarship is liable to obscure the
light of pastoral theology. If it is silly, to say the least, for
potentially good pastors to look at isolated latin texts from
Augustine without understanding the great themes of his
doctrine, it is ludicrous for serious lay people to plough
through a detailed commentary on Romans without any
conception of the practical implications of the doctrine
of grace, or without any picture of the fundamental trends
of New Testament studies today. If the theological college
set book degenerates into third-rate scholarship, the
parish "Bible class" sinks to eighth-rate scholarship. But
neither should be directly concerned with scholarship at
all; indirectly the best scholarship will be *used*, but the
subject should be approached by way of pastoral theology.

The mediator between these studies and Christian
practice is still prayer, pastoral theology implies prayer,

applied theology can only be used in the guidance of prayer. The most fundamental of all theological questions: "What does this doctrine mean in practice?" should more often be answered by an honest "nothing". The answer to: "What does this doctrine mean to prayer, and through prayer to life?" is always "something". Otherwise we are not dealing with the theology of an incarnational and redemptive religion.

In conclusion I must try to forestall an obvious criticism. It will be said that, for all my talk about pastoral and practical matters, we have still only a book, and a book which, if it claims no "scholarship", remains a mass of theory. All its talk about relations, chain-reactions, catalysts, and so on, is still far removed from Christian practice. We are back with the common complaint of pastors and perhaps more especially of their junior assistants, that all the theology they learned at their universities and theological colleges has no relevance to their pastoral work. The implication is that theology is useless, and if it has all been of the third-rate "scholarship" type perhaps it is. But the alternative possibility ought, in fairness, to be investigated: perhaps it is current pastoral practice that is useless? I believe this to be nearer the truth, and it throws up the importance of the negative use of theology: pastoral activity must be put to the theological test and ruthlessly eradicated if it fails.

An address delivered to a representative Christian audience which insisted on the centrality of prayer, on the importance of individual people, on the guidance of the faithful, on deep pastoral concern based on deep Christian principles: such would be received with re-sounding applause. An address delivered a week later to the same audience about the priority of evangelism, of Christian action, of social organisation—this, too, would receive resounding applause. But you cannot have *two* priorities! One must be relegated to second place: which? And why? The failure to answer this question, or even to ask it, lies at the heart of most of our pastoral difficulties especially since "evangelism" and "prayer" are words charged with emotional overtones which have drifted from their theological moorings.

My own claim is that this central dilemma can be submitted to the light of theology and answered beyond reasonable dispute. It can be briefly summed up in two equations: The priority of practical action—evangelism, social administration et cetera—backed up by prayer, equals heresy, frustration and failure. The centrality of prayer, guided by theology, issuing in practical action, equals orthodoxy, service and achievement. What is the substantiation for this view?

It is the "mixed life" of tradition, generally accepted as good, worthy and creative if "lower" than the contemplative life. The "active" life usually means much the same thing. If, to stretch a point, it covers the practical work of a layman living loyally, if not over-zealously, within the Church, then it is deemed conducive to his personal salvation. No orthodox pastoral theologian has ever faintly suggested that this "active" life can achieve more. It is therefore *not* truly evangelistic. Anything other than the centrality of prayer fails to uphold the doctrine of grace, and must take on the colour of Pelagianism. Prayer is response to grace, but prayer risks serious error unless it is supported by doctrine. We are back to the inviolable progression of prayer—theology—prayer—action, which is the theological basis of the Anglican ordinal.

There is no need to labour this point. But what is of subtler import to the contemporary position is that pastoral failure and frustration is due not to too much "evangelism" but to too much preoccupation with it and a failure to see the new theological depths of the modern meaning of the term. It is commonly assumed that an evangelistic approach *must* be "outward-looking", objective, unselfish, yet a Church may be so preoccupied with this one thing, interpreted far too narrowly, that it turns in on itself as unhealthily as if its overriding concern was spirituality, canon law, or liturgy. Preoccupation is a bad thing in all cases: preoccupation with prayer, or with theology, lead to the same introversion, the same "tension", which militates against healthy prayer and sound theology themselves. Yet it is, in fact, preoccupation with this pseudo-evangelism which controls almost the whole of present-day pastoral practice; which takes up the time by which prayer and reading are squeezed out. It is time, therefore, that we faced some of the modern pastoral theological facts which impinge on this problem.

What exactly do we mean by "evangelism"? The gospel means the manifestation of the glory of God in Christ, and his offer of salvation and glory to men. But men are indissociable from the whole universe, so the gospel can be concerned with nothing less than the eschatological hope that God shall be all in all. In a startlingly "modern" text which contemporary pastors seen to have forgotten, St. Mark cites our Lord as commanding the gospel to be preached, not to all men but to all the creation. We are back with E. L. Mascall and Teilhard de Chardin, and indeed with St. Francis. His preaching to the birds was no childishly literal response to Christ's command but a deeply contemplative obedience: it was a union of love with creation. Such contemplative harmony, such eucharistic lifting up of creation into the redemptive stream is, therefore, an essential prerequisite for "evangelism". However "outward-looking" we may be, however healthily athirst for converts, some elementary form of contemplative prayer must have the priority.

Nevertheless, creation implies people, for they are its priests; it is through men that the glory of God in creation becomes articulate. Therefore, according to St. Matthew, we are to "make disciples" of all the nations as a corollary to proclaiming the gospel to the whole creation (Matt. 13. 51–2, 27. 57, 28. 19). All the scholars agree that to "make disciples" is a technical term peculiar to St. Matthew, and it means very much more than "to recruit", or even "to convert". It means to "give understanding to", or, in I. T. Ramsey's phraseology "to prepare for a cosmic disclosure". In down to earth pastoral terms it can mean no less than to guide in prayer. Linguistic philosophy alone makes it perfectly clear that, in these days (if in any other days) this cannot be achieved by *talking*.

Pastoral-theology has to be theological, but it also has to face the facts of a particular situation. And the one, all-enveloping, and irrefragable modern fact is that we no longer live in "Christendom". Twelve years ago I tried to construct a system of pastoral polity which faced up to this fact: let me repeat for perhaps the thousandth time that the "remnant concept" is not an alternative to evangelism but a method of achieving it. Since then, I think I can claim considerable support for this approach, however inadequate my original hypothesis. In *Paul and The Salvation of Mankind*, Johannes Munck has thoroughly exploded the popular pastoral view that St. Paul was the exemplar of mass evangelism in the modern sense. He was rather, according to Munck's convincing thesis, concerned with eschatology, with the consummation of creation in glory. And as preliminary to this, his task was to win the 'first-fruits" of all the nations, which was to rebound towards the salvation of the Jews: to St. Paul, evangelism was a most subtle thing, depending upon and working through small local Churches. It is also of some interest that Munck discounts the theory which sees Paul as a "theologian", that is as a scholar, and makes him into very much what I have defined as a pastoral theologian.

The bold rejection of "Christendom", as both fact and immediate ideal, force the acceptance of "secularity", first as fact, and secondly as something still within the purview of divine providence. Karl Rahner superbly sums up what I have been trying to say: "If we once have the courage to give up our defence of the old façades which have nothing or very little behind them; if we cease to maintain, in public, the pretence of a universal Christendom; if we stop straining every nerve to get *everybody* baptised, to get *everybody* married in church and on to our registers (even when success means only, at bottom, a victory for tradition, custom and ancestry, not for true faith and interior conviction); if, by letting all this go, we visibly relieve Christianity of the burdensome impression that it accepts responsibility for everything that goes on under this Christian top-dressing, the impression that Christianity is *natura sua* a sort of Everyman's Religious Varnish, a folk-religion (at the same level as that of folk-costumes)—*then* we can be free for real missionary adventure and apostolic self-confidence." (*Mission and Grace*, vol. I, pp. 50–1.)

Now *if* we have the courage to be done with Christendom once and for all two sets of possibilities arise. We are rid of a great deal of superfluous and artificial "parish work", the whole of which is pointless except as Everyman's Religious Varnish, and we are therefore freed for an adventurous search by way of prayer and pastoral theology. There is some positive light thrown upon the present situation: "evangelism" in the sense of an attempt to claim all people for the Church as soon as possible, with everything geared to this one end, is shown up to be not too ambitious but far too narrow a concept.

The concept of "secularity" becomes a blessing in disguise if only for leading us back to a serious considera-tion of the doctrine of creation, and the unifying contem-plation which is the only Christian, and evangelistic, approach to it. Professor Leonard Hodgson has recently written: "Consider some of the effects of realising that to be a committed Christian is to share our Lord's vision of the world as our heavenly Father's world, to share in his devotion to God's care for the welfare of his Creatures. God, we say in our creed, is maker of all things visible and invisible . . . If to be a committed Christian is to see the world, and try to live, in this way, the primary task of the Church and of us clergy will be to encourage our fellow men to do so. This, rather than the acceptance of Christ as personal Saviour, will be, in the first instance, what we shall mean by conversion." (*The Expository Times*, Sep-tember 1966, pp. 363–4.) The article continues with both illustration and substantiation of what I have tried to describe as the pastoral theological process: "The attempt to understand the actual conditions of life in the world of today, the willingness to learn about it from those who are subject to its pressures, will be as important for us as the study of the insights of theologians in the past. Not that these can be neglected. From them we have learned what is still, and I believe will always be, the core of the Christian gospel . . . There will be reality in the sanctuary when those who come to worship are there because their attempt to do the Father's work has taught them their need of communion with the living Lord."

Rahner's "*if*" is still a formidable obstacle, but it is hopeful that this pastoral theological approach to the world is at least in the air. The problem which remains to be solved is the relation between the Church and the secular world, which has to be faced so soon as Christen-dom is rejected. And there appear to be two conflicting views. On the one hand there are those who wish to blur the distinction, or even to obliterate it: in its extreme forms this is represented by the "secular gospel", the "religionless Christianity", the "non-Church", and the "death of God" schools of thought. I think this kind of approach must fail for the rather surprising reason that, however radical, vogueish and *avant garde* it may appear to be, it is really out of date. It is, in fact, and no doubt to the surprise of its champions, medieval, because it remains subtly tinged with the Christendom concept. With its rejection of the dogmatic, the metaphysical, with spiritual and ascetical discipline, the motive behind the movement appears only to embrace as many people as possible under the Christian banner. I have no doubt that many of those who think in this way are genuinely concerned to reinterpret the gospel in contemporary terms, which is a worthy aim. But its inevitable consequence is to stretch and strain at the faith so as to make it not so much contemporary but acceptable. To harness modern thought to the faith is one thing: it is pastoral theology. To harness the faith to modern thought is quite another. It is significant that all these so-called "modern" schools of thought —the "non-Church", the "death of God" and all the rest—are the products of the misunderstanding of and preoccupation with "evangelism". It is also curious that the so-called "practical evangelist", he who *restricts* the Church's redemptive work to the proclamation of the gospel, is siding with the most narrow academician. For both assume that there is but one type of theology with but one immediate function; all is straight theology to be accepted or rejected, and that is the end of the matter. I strongly reiterate that this first function of theology is of great importance, the bold proclamation of revealed truth to the world gives theology its value amongst the autonomous pluralities of a secular culture. That theology functions does not render it subservient to the pragmatic test. But both of these attitudes are far too narrow: the theological function of proclamation, of speaking to the world in truth, becomes enriched by its association with other, more subtle functions.

On the other side of the fence are those who, admitting the secular and rejecting Christendom, nevertheless wish to accentuate the distinction; to emphasise an efficient *diaspora* Church by tightening discipline and instilling a remnant integrity and zeal. With the modern insistence that theological understanding is only possible through the eyes of faith, that it demands spiritual insight and discernment, this latter interpretation is the only one which can stand up to theological investigation. But in pastoral activity I wonder whether a creative compromise is not possible? Amongst other things, the champions of the former ideal rebel against narrow ecclesiasticism, pietism, regimentation, and the kind of arrogant authoritarianism which frustrates personal liberty and experiment. It dislikes religious convention and that unloving austerity that so often goes with it. On this few would disagree.

Would it not be a workable compromise to accept the real and inevitable distinction between the Church and secular society while doing all we reasonably can to keep it secret? May we look forward in confidence to the day when the Church gives itself selflessly to the service of God and society, not least by a contemplative love for creation which lifts everything into the redemptive stream? May we look forward to the time when the Church quietly gets on with its real job and stops talking? That will only be possible when we have got rid of pseudo-evangelism and when we have rediscovered the real thing. And that will only be possible when we have rediscovered the manifold uses of theology and remarried it to prayer. Albeit deposed by a secular culture, and dethroned by the *diaspora* situation, the queen of the sciences is still our most reliable guide; not only in the lives of Christians but in the Church's unique and ultimate service of the world.

Index